Louisa May Alcott

WHO WROTE THAT?

WHO
WROTE
THAT?

Louisa May Alcott

Elizabeth Silverthorne

Chelsea House Publishers
Philadelphia

CHELSEA HOUSE PUBLISHERS

EDITOR IN CHIEF Sally Cheney
DIRECTOR OF PRODUCTION Kim Shinners
CREATIVE MANAGER Takeshi Takahashi
MANUFACTURING MANAGER Diann Grasse

STAFF FOR LOUISA MAY ALCOTT

ASSOCIATE EDITOR Benjamin Kim
PICTURE RESEARCHER Jane Sanders
PRODUCTION ASSISTANT Jaimie Winkler
SERIES AND COVER DESIGNER Keith Trego
LAYOUT 21st Century Publishing and Communications, Inc.

http://www.chelseahouse.com

3 5 7 9 8 6 4 2

Library of Congress Cataloging-in-Publication Data

CIP applied for ISBN 0-7910-6721-1

Table of Contents

Louisa May Alcott in 1875. Her family provided the inspiration for her stories of the March sisters and her life was filled with both the turbulent events of the Civil War and the ideas of progressive thinkers such as Emerson and Thoreau.

Jo March and Louisa Alcott

"Never liked girls or knew many, except my sisters. But our experiences may prove interesting, though I doubt it."
—Louisa May Alcott Journals

NEITHER LOUISA MAY Alcott nor her publisher was enthusiastic about the "girls' book" she was writing. In their wildest imaginings they could not have dreamed that *Little Women* would become one of the most popular juvenile books ever written—or that in 1995 it would appear on the bestseller list of the *New York Times*. No one could have made them believe that for over 130 years it would remain a beloved favorite, despite the modern advancements that have taken place since that time.

Why do we who live in the computer age still enjoy reading about the daily lives of Meg, Jo, Beth, and Amy who grew up in New England in the mid-1800s without telephones, radios or television? What still fascinates us about these girls who never wore blue jeans, listened to CD's, watched movies, or rode in a car? The answer, of course, is that they seem as real as our own neighbors. And the reason they are so realistic is that they are based on the real family of Louisa May Alcott. The personalities and activities of Meg, Jo, Beth, and Amy March and their friends and relatives in *Little Women* mirror the personalities and activities of Anna, Louisa, Lizzie, and May Alcott and their friends and relatives in real life. Though many things can change through the years—language, ways of traveling, and entertainment—human nature remains the same. Growing up still has its happy times and its sad times, its good days and its bad days. No matter what our surroundings, we still have to struggle to develop our talents and to overcome our weaknesses. Reading about how others make it through the ups and downs of life can be helpful and even fascinating when the characters are as lively and interesting as the March sisters.

Throughout *Little Women* the girls wrestle with the same weaknesses that plagued Alcott and her sisters. Meg (based on Anna, the oldest sister) wrestles with envy and sometimes vanity. Beth (based on Elizabeth) is handicapped by excessive timidity and is overly sensitive. Amy (based on May) is often selfish and self-centered. And Jo—like her creator, Louisa—is impulsive and rebellious, and her recklessness often gets her into trouble.

Marmee, the mother in *Little Women*, is very like Abigail (or Abba, as she was known), the mother who was the warm, loving heart of the Alcott household. Abba May Alcott was the daughter of Colonel Joseph May of Boston, who was well-known for both his generosity and for his quick temper. Abba inherited both qualities and passed them along to her second daughter. When Louisa's temper ran out of control, she often blamed it on her "peppery" May ancestors.

Her mother understood how hard it was for Louisa to be patient and obedient, and gave her rebellious daughter constant loving encouragement. Probably because they were so much alike, Louisa and her mother were extremely close. As she grew up, Louisa realized how difficult life was for Abba, and she had hardly entered her teens before her chief goal in life became to earn enough money to make life more easy and comfortable for her hardworking, self-sacrificing mother.

The Alcott girls also adored their father, but Amos Bronson Alcott was a strange and controversial man for his time—or perhaps for any time. He was a man of grand ideas, an educator and a philosopher who won the respect and friendship of such outstanding men as Ralph Waldo Emerson and Henry David Thoreau. His ideas on education were so far ahead of his time that only very recently have we begun to make use of some of them.

He was a gifted speaker and his lectures were well received, but he had little practical sense and earning money was not among his priorities or talents.

While she was still very young Louisa realized that her beloved father would never be a reliable breadwinner. After she became a writer, she often thought of doing a biography of her father, but she never felt able to do it other than in the form of a long poem about his life. In

Little Women she also found the character of the father difficult to handle, so she sent him off to take part in the Civil War, leaving Marmee to struggle (like Abba) with the problem of raising four daughters alone and on very little income.

The Pilgrim's Progress by John Bunyan was Bronson Alcott's favorite book, and both the Alcott sisters and their counterparts in *Little Women* grew up under its influence. The pilgrim in the book is a man named Christian, who travels through the world trying to reach the Celestial City (Heaven). On the way he meets many temptations, such as the town of Vanity Fair, and many dangers, including the Slough of Despond and the Giant Despair. A favorite game of the young Alcott sisters was to make up plays acting out the stories in *The Pilgrim's Progress*, and Louisa continued to reread the book all through her life, finding inspiration in the simple beauty of the language, the vivid characters, the humor, and Bunyan's reverent feeling for nature.

Despite hard times, sickness, and poverty, a spirit of fun and adventure was usually present in the Alcott and March homes. Pillow fights on Saturday nights were a weekly tradition. The girls in their long white night-gowns would race through the house, pounding each other and their father with pillows until they were exhausted, at which point they would say their prayers and fall into bed. (In *Little Men* Louisa describes the same kind of weekly pillow fights at Plumfield School.) There were lots of family jokes, laughter and games, but above all, there was a sense of caring for each other that outweighed any petty quarrelling. Like the March sisters in *Little Women*, the Alcott sisters fought and sometimes played mean tricks on each other. But always they forgave and forgot and renewed their affectionate relationships.

A still from the 1994 movie adaptation of Little Women. *Even today, the novel's appeal remains as enduring as ever.*

Mrs. Alcott set the example of sustaining love by her unshakable devotion to her visionary husband. No matter how frustrated she must have been by his lack of concern about the necessity for money to support a growing family, she always supported his right to live by his beliefs. In her journal she wrote, "Mr. Alcott cannot bring himself to work for gain; but we have not yet learned to live without money or means." But she also wrote that she could not live without him. "I think I can as easily learn to live without breath," she said.

Although Louisa and her sisters felt the same devotion to their impractical father, they came to realize how difficult his way of life made theirs. As an adult, Louisa once humorously described a philosopher as "A man up in a balloon, with his family and friends holding the ropes which confine him to earth and trying to haul him down."

The father in *Little Women* is a minister who, like Bronson Alcott, lives in a rather dreamy world, detached from practical everyday life.

One of the themes running through *Little Women* is that no matter how little a person has, he or she can always find a way to help those who have even less. Abba's father had instilled this ideal in her, and her husband Branson believed in it even more fervently. Together, mainly by example, they impressed upon the young Alcott sisters the importance of sharing with those less fortunate. In the second chapter of *Little Women* Louisa used this idea in the scene in which the Marches give their eagerly anticipated Christmas breakfast to a poorer family.

Growing up in prim and proper Victorian times, both Louisa and Jo often shocked their more conventional friends and neighbors. Jo's impulsive, reckless behavior faithfully depicts Louisa's harum-scarum ways. Both Louisa and Jo often got into scrapes and frequently had to pay the price for rash actions, and both sincerely regretted and tried to atone for any grief they caused others.

The writing careers of Jo and Louisa are similar. Each begins as a young writer by selling stories she knows are "rubbishy" but which bring in a little much-needed income from cheap magazines. Both of them also go on to write bigger and better works. Like Louisa, Jo gets more pleasure from buying things for her family than in spending on herself. She is tremendously happy to be able to pay for "groceries and gowns," a new carpet, and a vacation at the seashore for Marmee and Beth.

After the huge success of *Little Women*, the Alcotts never again suffered from want. Fans and publishers demanded more of the same kind of book, and Louisa wrote and wrote and wrote. Eventually what came to be called the "Little Women Series" grew to eight books, including *Little Men*, *An Old-Fashioned Girl*, *Eight Cousins*, *Rose in Bloom*, *Under the Lilacs*, *Jack and Jill*, and *Jo's Boys*. Louisa was able to supply her parents with comforts as well as send her sister May to Europe to study art, help her widowed sister Anna take care of her two boys, and provide for May's daughter Lulu after May died.

A number of movies and videos of *Little Women* have brought the characters to life on the screen and have continually renewed interest in the book throughout the years. In 2001 the Houston Grand Opera performed a musical version of the book, which was shown on television. Children in England, France, Holland, Japan and other countries have shared the enthusiasm of American children for reading about the lives of Meg, Jo, Beth, and Amy, the four sisters who lived in such a different

Did you know...

At least six movie versions of *Little Women* have been made.

world so long ago. The book that the author doubted would be of much interest shows no signs of fading away, and Louisa May Alcott continues to live on in the character of Jo March.

Bronson Alcott in front of his school, the Concord School of Philosophy, which was opened in 1879. Until then, his ideas on education were far too advanced for most people to take seriously.

Runaway

"Running away was one of the delights of my early days; and I still enjoy sudden flights out of the nest to look about this very interesting world, and then go back to report."

—Louisa May Alcott

ON NOVEMBER 29, 1832, Bronson Alcott wrote to his father-in-law, Colonel Joseph May, to announce the birth of Louisa May, the second daughter in the Alcott family. It also happened to be Bronson's thirty-third birthday. She is a robust baby, he proudly told Colonel May, adding, "she has a fine foundation for health and energy of character."

Baby Louisa had the dark hair and brown eyes of the May family rather than the light hair and blue eyes of the Alcott family. And before long her father was to discover that she did indeed have "energy of character"; in fact, as he noted in his journal, she was a "willful" child. Many parents in the mid-nineteenth century felt it was their duty to teach their children to be submissive and obedient by using harsh punishments. "Spare the rod and spoil the child" was a familiar saying. Abigail and Bronson Alcott believed in gentler ways of training their children. They did it by making them *want* to be good, so their consciences would be clear and they would feel that they were lovable. Unfortunately, this method of training also led to frequent feelings of guilt when they did not live up to the standards expected of them.

At the time of Louisa's birth the Alcotts were living in Germantown, a suburb of Philadelphia, where Bronson had established a school at the request of Quaker friends. When Bronson's chief backer died and the school enrollment began to dwindle, he moved the family to the city of Philadelphia, where another experimental school soon failed. Moving back to Boston and starting over there seemed a promising idea. In July of 1834, the Alcotts sold most of their possessions to pay their debts. Then they packed what was left, said goodbye to good friends they had made, and with their two small daughters, Anna and Louisa, boarded a steamer headed for Boston.

It was not long after they had set sail when Louisa disappeared. After a frantic search of the ship (and no doubt fervent prayers that she was still on board) she was discovered in the engine room. She was covered with coal dust and black grease and blissfully unaware of the alarm she had caused. Apparently the sights and sounds and smells of the lower regions of the ship with its glowing fires, strange smells and huge steel shafts moving back and forth had attracted the toddler. This excursion was only the first of many scrapes young Louisa's curiosity would lead her into.

The slow pace of life in Germantown contrasted sharply with the hustle and bustle of life in Boston. Tall-masted ships from around the world delivered goods that were taken to market in horse drawn wagons that sometimes clogged the busy streets along the wharfs. Rows of red brick houses lined the cobbled streets. The Common, a large public park in the heart of Boston, soon became Louisa's favorite place in the city. Here she could play in the grass, sail paper boats in the Frog Pond, and rest in the shade of the tall elm trees, watching elegant ladies ride by in carriages and listening to the cries of vendors who pushed carts filled with fruit and pies. From time to time the town crier strode by, ringing his bell and telling the news of the day.

Louisa was fascinated by her father's school in the Masonic Temple near the Common. His classroom didn't look like the usual classroom of that day. Decorated with busts and pictures of important writers and thinkers, it was filled with sunlight. The chairs for the students were arranged on the colorful carpet in a semi-circle around the teacher's desk. Instead of lecturing and requiring his students to memorize facts and figures, Bronson engaged them in lively discussions about their bodies and souls, encouraging them to think and express their ideas. His assistant was Elizabeth Peabody, a brilliant young woman who would later become famous for opening the first kindergarten in the United States (in Boston) and for organizing public and private kindergartens in other places. The Alcott's third daughter, Elizabeth, who was born in June of 1835, was named after this outstanding educator.

Essayist and thinker Ralph Waldo Emerson, a good friend of the Alcotts and one of Louisa's childhood crushes. He and Bronson shared many views on education and philosophy and Emerson was one of the key figures in the Transcendentalism movement.

Bronson's Temple School in Boston continued for five years. During its first years people interested in new ways of education enthusiastically praised it, and important visitors from abroad sometimes arrived for visits. One day, Louisa was watching the lessons as she liked to do, trying to be quiet so she would not be hushed or asked to leave, when she saw a tall, thin man talking with her father. The man had a serene, kindly expression that warmed her heart. She was told he was Ralph Waldo Emerson, but she had no inkling that he would become a very important a friend of the Alcott family, or that he would be the most influential man in her life next to her father.

Mrs. Alcott took every opportunity to impress three rules for living on her young daughters. They were:

1. Rule yourself.
2. Love your neighbor.
3. Hope, and keep busy.

Louisa never forgot the lesson she learned on her fourth birthday, which was celebrated in her father's schoolroom. As "queen of the day" she wore a crown of flowers and stood on a table to give a little plum cake to each child as they marched past. By some oversight, there was one more child than the number of cakes. She saw that if she gave away the last cake, there would be none for her. As the birthday queen she felt she should have it and held on to it tightly until her mother, who was in charge of music at the school, reminded her that it was better to give away than to keep nice things, adding, "I know my Louy will not let the little friend go without." Louisa gave the plummy cake to the friend and received a kiss and her "first lesson in the sweetness of self-denial."

One day when her mother was busy at the school, the adventurous Louisa set out to explore Boston on her own. For a long time she wandered through the streets, stopping to play with some Irish children who shared a meal of cold potatoes, salt fish and bread crusts with her. Finally she realized she was tired and tried to find her way home. When she couldn't remember the way, she sat down on the steps of a house. After resting her head on the back of a big, friendly dog, she watched the lamplighter until she could keep her eyes open no longer, and she fell asleep. It was twilight when the ringing bell and booming voice of the town crier awakened her. "Lost!" he shouted. "A little girl, six years old, in a pink frock, white hat, and new green shoes."

"Why, that's me!" Louisa called to him.

The town crier took her to his home where his wife fed her bread and molasses while her family was sent for. The next day Louisa had time to think about the worry her recklessness had caused while she spent several hours tied by a string to the arm of a sofa. It wouldn't be the last time her curiosity would get her into trouble, and it would be one of the many incidents from her childhood that she used in her books. In *Little Men*, the tomboy Nan suffers a similar punishment for getting lost by straying away from her playmates.

Sometimes it was Louisa's generous spirit that also got her into trouble. By the time she was seven she had learned well the lesson of sharing whatever we have with those less fortunate. On a visit to family friends in Providence, she met some poor children who she thought were hungry. Impulsively she ran to the kitchen, which happened to be vacant, and without asking permission, took food for her new friends. When she received a scolding instead of the praise she expected, she was astonished and deeply hurt.

Living in Boston during these early years, Louisa came to know some of the family relatives. Her grandfather, Colonel Joseph May, shared the strict Victorian ideas that children should be "seen but not heard" unless they were spoken to. He expected a standard of behavior—especially of being good and quiet—that was hard for Louisa to meet. But even when he frowned at her noisiness or naughtiness, she knew he loved all his grandchildren, and he was always generous with them.

Her mother's brother, Samuel J. May, was a Unitarian

minister. He was the one who had introduced Bronson to Abba, and he remained a true and helpful friend to the family. As she grew older, Louisa would come to admire her Uncle Samuel for his courage and energy in the antislavery movement. Cousin Lizzie Wells would also prove to be a lifelong helpful friend to the family and especially to Louisa, who as an adult often turned to her in times of trouble.

The spirit of "Aunt Hancock," Abba Alcott's great-aunt, still hung over the family, although Louisa probably never met this legendary relative who was quite old by the time Abba and Bronson married. Her first name was Dorothy, but she insisted on being called Aunt Hancock, using the name of her famous first husband, John Hancock, whose bold signature tops the list of the signers of the Declaration of Independence. When her husband became the first Governor of Massachusetts, she was an imperious First Lady. Bronson often told his daughters of being summoned to dinner with Aunt Hancock when she learned that their mother was engaged to a schoolteacher. Sitting in her thronelike chair, she told him stories calculated to impress him with the days when she had reigned as the Governor's Lady on Beacon Hill. At dinner, they would begin with dessert, as Aunt Hancock said that was the traditional way, and she would not put up with the new-fangled idea of having dessert at the end of the meal. And she carved the roast

> ### *Did you know...*
>
> Each Alcott sister, like each March sister in *Little Women*, had a special talent: Anna (Meg) for acting; Louisa (Jo) for writing; Lizzie (Beth) for music; and May (Amy) for painting.

beef herself. Bronson saw through her pretentiousness to the good heart underneath, and in the end they got along very well. Although Louisa said there was no real-life model for Aunt March in *Little Women*, it seems likely that, either consciously or unconsciously, she modeled that bossy, tart-tongued but generous old lady on her Aunt Hancock.

Louisa said that she became an abolitionist at an early age when she heard her father speak sympathetically about men who were punished for actively insisting that slavery should be abolished. An incident that reinforced her feelings of sympathy for blacks happened during one of her runaway scrapes. One day while she and her mother were walking on the Common, she escaped momentarily from her mother's watchful eye and fell into the Frog Pond. Gasping for breath and unable to free herself, she knew she was about to drown when suddenly a strange, dark face appeared above her, and she felt strong arms lifting her out of the water. The Negro boy who had seen her situation had come to her aid quicker than any of the bystanders who stood watching in horror. He quickly slipped away before she could learn his name, but she often expressed gratitude for his action and often mentioned it as proof of the kindliness of his race.

Another memorable experience connected with slavery occurred during her childhood. She was in a kitchen that had a large brick oven with an iron door beside the open fireplace. Hearing a noise in the oven, she ran over and opened the door. Looking out at her was a thin, black face with frightened eyes. Quickly slamming the door, she went to find her mother, who explained that the man was a runaway slave from a Southern plantation who was being hidden until he could be taken to Canada where he would be free. Louisa must never say a word about what she had seen, her mother warned, for if he were caught, he and the ones who had hidden him would be punished.

Louisa was seven when her father's Boston Temple School closed. During its final years of operation, the number of enrolled students had been dwindling. Since

Bronson encouraged the students to talk freely about their bodies and how they interacted with their minds and feelings (even discussing the miracle of birth with them), the rumor went around that he was teaching sex education. This idea shocked some of the parents. Many of them also did not like the idea that an abolitionist was teaching their children. The final straw for them was when Bronson admitted a little black girl to the school, insisting it should be open to all children. After that, indignant parents yanked their children out until the enrollment dropped so low that the school could not be kept open.

The famous thinker and writer Ralph Waldo Emerson had become Bronson's close friend. They shared the same ideas about the need for progressive education, the necessity of doing away with slavery, and the importance of each person's learning to rely on his own conscience as his guide in life. Both Emerson and Alcott felt that Bronson's efforts to change the way of educating children had been misunderstood. Emerson thought if his friend could live in a quiet, natural setting away from the city, he would have time to think and write and perhaps make important contributions to the world of ideas. He urged Bronson to move the family to his hometown, the little village of Concord.

With Emerson's help, Bronson arranged to rent a cottage in Concord, which was located about twenty miles from Boston. It was here Louisa began the years that she would later recall as the happiest of her life. As they left Boston to begin the three-hour coach ride to their new home in April of 1840, Abba noticed that her seven-year-old daughter was recording all the details of the journey in a notebook. The budding writer had already begun her career.

Henry David Thoreau, who was friends with the Alcott family, was a poet and naturalist who wrote the essay Walden *and other works extolling the virtues of living within nature and other progressive ideas.*

3

Tomboy

"I scrambled up to childhood out of which I fell with a crash into girlhood & continued falling over fences, out of trees, up hill and downstairs, tumbling from one year to the next til the topsey turvey girl shot up into a topsey turvey woman . . . ."
—Louisa May Alcott

QUIET CONCORD WAS very different from busy Boston. White houses and churches dotted green lawns, and meadows behind the houses ran down to the peaceful Concord River. The cottage that the Alcotts rented from Edmund Hosmer for $52 a year had a large garden and a porch that opened into four large rooms. But the best things of all to Louisa were the wide-open spaces where she could run as much as she liked. When she was grown she said, "I always thought I must have been a deer or a horse in some former state, because it was such a joy to run. No boy could be my friend till I had beaten him in a race, and no girl if she refused to climb fences, and be a tomboy."

The Alcott girls found playmates among the village children. A boy named Cy liked to tease Louisa and egg her into doing risky things. One day he dared her to jump off a high beam in his barn. She did and sprained both ankles and had to be carried home on a board. Another time Cy bet Louisa she wouldn't rub red peppers in her eyes to "see how it felt." Of course she did and suffered the consequences of red, burning, teary eyes. When they were grown, she and Cy remained friends and laughed about their daredevil childhood.

During their first summer in the Hosmer Cottage a new sister was born—a pretty, golden-haired baby named May. Anna took it as her special duty to watch over and help take care of May. Everyone in the family worked. As soon as a child was strong enough, Abba would teach her how to clean and cook and sew.

Housework was not easy in the mid-1800s. Dishes had to be washed and dried by hand; clothes and linens had to be rubbed on scrub boards, rinsed, and hung on lines to dry; lamps had to be cleaned, furniture dusted, floors swept and scrubbed; ashes from stoves and fireplaces had to be swept up; and the wood that cooked their food and warmed the house had to be carried into the house from the woodshed. Their father needed help in weeding the vegetable garden he had planted—and since he did not believe in eating the flesh of animals, it was a large one.

The little house was very bare. There was not even a stove, so all their cooking was done in the fireplace. Their meals were plain and meager, consisting mainly of porridge, fruit and vegetables, coarse bread and milk. A friend who came to visit later wrote that while she was there, the Alcotts were eating only two meals a day and giving the third meal to a family even poorer than they were. During the winter when there was no fresh produce to be had, they lived mostly on apples and squash.

Mr. Alcott worked on neighboring farms as a farmhand and chopped wood for a dollar a day. Winters were terribly cold, and it took a lot of wood to keep the temperature in the house above freezing. Mrs. Alcott was greatly concerned that the children might suffer from the cold, and her impractical husband's cheerful assurances that everything would be all right did not convince her. On a snowy evening when the woodshed was nearly empty, she was greatly relieved when a kind neighbor sent over a load of wood. Then Bronson came tromping in and announced that he had given the wood to a family with a sick baby and helped them carry it away in a wheelbarrow. Abba must have been ready to scream. What about his own family and baby! Just then another neighbor arrived with another load of wood. "I told you we would not suffer," Bronson said.

After the first harsh winter, the coming of spring seemed full of joyful promise. When the children found a half-starved robin in the garden, they carefully warmed and fed it, and eight-year-old Louisa wrote a poem about it entitled "To the First Robin":

To the First Robin

Welcome, welcome, little stranger,
Fear no harm, and fear no danger;
We are glad to see you here,
For you sing "Sweet Spring is near."

Now the white snow melts away;
Now the flowers blossom gay:
Come dear bird and build your nest,
For we love our robin best.

Their father was the girls' first teacher, and he often made learning fun. To teach them the letters of the alphabet, he performed gymnastics. For the letter "I" he stood up very stiff and tall and stalked around the room. For "X" he lay on the floor with his arms and legs spread wide. The letter "S" was represented by contorting his body and hissing like a goose. In *Little Women*, Grandfather March uses the same game to teach his grandchildren the alphabet.

The Pilgrim's Progress was a favorite bedtime book. The stories of Christian's journey read so dramatically by their father became a part of the little Alcotts' thinking. They often imagined they were pilgrims making their way through life bearing packs of their sins on their backs. They also made up games using characters from the book such as Obstinate, Mrs. Much-afraid and Mr. Ready-to-halt, and places such as Vanity Fair and the Delectable Mountains. In *Little Women*, Meg, Jo, Beth, and Amy also thought of themselves as pilgrims trying to reach the Celestial City.

Although the Alcott girls knew their mother was often anxious and worried, they did not understand the dire poverty in which they lived. Nor did they understand that their family was dependent on the charity of kind neighbors (especially Mr. Emerson) and some of their mother's relatives. The country was in a depression, and times were hard. In Philadelphia, people lined up to receive free soup, and in Boston, beggars roamed the streets. And still Bronson insisted they would be all right if he could only convince people to live according to his ideas.

Some of his ideas were connected with a way of thinking called "transcendentalism" that became popular among writers and thinkers in New England in the middle 1800s. Transcendentalists believed that each person has insight (an invisible spirit) that can reveal the truth about the world better than their senses or experiences can. Bronson's friend, Ralph

Waldo Emerson, was an outstanding spokesman for the movement. He understood and approved Bronson's teaching methods, which were based on the belief that it is more important to teach the virtues of honesty and unselfishness and to impress children with the necessity of constantly examining their consciences than it is to cram their heads with facts and figures.

People in old England apparently appreciated Bronson's ideas on education more than people in New England did. The English named a school after him and invited him to come to England to visit it. The whole family was excited—surely something good would happen as a result of this trip. Something did happen, but it was not at all what they expected. When their father arrived home, he brought along three strangers—two men and a boy. Bronson happily introduced Mr. Charles Lane, his son William and Mr. Henry Wright, all from England. The new arrivals were to live in the cottage with them for the winter, and when spring came they would all start a new life together—according to a splendid new plan of Bronson's.

After a cramped winter in the cottage, their number was reduced by one as Mr. Wright found the scanty diet and crowded conditions not to his taste and left the group. Despite Mr. Wright's departure, Bronson's great experiment could still be put into practice. The plan was for the Alcotts, the Lanes, and any others who shared their ideals to live and work together in peace and harmony, sharing everything. They would be more concerned with their spirits than with their bodies, dressing plainly and eating a vegetarian diet.

With Emerson's help, the Alcotts bought an old farmhouse and 100 acres of land about fifteen miles from Concord. The house was halfway up a steep hill with wild woods behind it. They called it Fruitlands—more hopefully than realistically, as there were no orchards whatsoever on the grounds when they moved in. Downstairs were three large rooms connected by steep, narrow stairways to the sleeping quarters under the low eaves. On June 1, 1843, ten-year-old Louisa rode along in the wooden wagon that carried her family to their new home.

At the time of the move, she began writing a daily journal, a habit she would keep up for the rest of her life. Everyone in the Alcott family kept journals; Bronson considered it an important teaching tool in learning to express ideas and emotions. The children freely wrote their thoughts and feelings even though they knew their parents would read the journals and comment on what they read there. Louisa liked writing in her journals, and happily for our understanding of her, many of them have survived. Because of the journals we know exactly how she felt about many things at Fruitlands.

She definitely did not like Mr. Lane as her teacher, nor the "fussy" woman who came to teach music. She didn't enjoy cooking and washing, but did her chores as well as she could to help her mother. She enjoyed husking corn, which was like a game to her. She didn't mind bathing in cold water or object to the diet, which consisted of porridge, coarse bread, and water for breakfast; bread, vegetables, and water at noon; and bread, water, and fruit in the evening. Members of the commune avoided dairy products, believing that animals should not be "enslaved," and avoided wearing cotton as it was produced by the slave labor of humans.

What she enjoyed most was racing up the hill behind the house, running in the fields pretending to be a horse or a bird, picking berries, teasing William Lane, and playing make-believe games with her sisters. In the evenings she liked to read stories by Charles Dickens, or a book called *The Vicar of Wakefield*. Sometimes she memorized poetry, which she recited to herself as she was going to sleep.

Louisa's journal records her struggle to "rule herself" and control her temper. "As I went to bed the moon came up very brightly and looked at me. I felt sad because I have been cross today, and did not mind Mother. I cried, and then I felt better." Another time she wrote, "I was cross today, and I cried when I went to sleep. I made good resolutions, and felt better in my heart. If I only *kept* all I make I should be the best girl in the world. But I don't, and so am very bad."

On October 8, which was her mother's birthday, Louisa's first thought when she woke was "I must be very good." She gave her mother a moss cross and wrote a poem for her. In her journal that evening she wrote, "I wish I was rich, I was good, and we were all a happy family this day."

Louisa was old enough to see that life at Fruitlands was hardest on her mother. The men often took time out to have long, philosophical discussions or went off on teaching missions. But Abba's work never ended, and the constant effort to keep everyone fed, the house clean, and the clothes washed and ironed was wearing her down. One day when the men had gone off to a conference, Fruitlands' main crop would have been destroyed were it not for the frantic efforts of Mrs. Alcott and the children. The barley had been cut and stacked to dry when a violent northeaster storm threatened. Calling to the children to bring baskets and bags, she snatched sheets from her pine chest and spread them on the ground. The children rushed back and forth dumping their baskets of barley onto the sheets which were then dragged into the barn. They managed to get most of the grain safely under the roof of the barn before the storm broke, and although their legs trembled with weariness and were scratched by the hard stubble, they were pleased with their effort.

From time to time newcomers joined the Fruitlands community, but most of them left after a short stay. Others, like a woman who was expelled for eating fish, were asked to leave. It took more self-sacrifice and more patience than most humans have to live in the kind of Eden that Alcott and Lane were trying to create. As winter came on, even they realized their plan was failing, and they hunted desperately for a way to save it. Across the river was a community of people called Shakers who lived in a village where they all shared the work and owned all the property in common. Maybe, thought Bronson, Fruitlands could use the Shaker village as a model and survive.

The trouble with that idea was that the Shakers did not believe in families. In their village, the men lived in one building and the women in another. Orphans, turned over to them by the government, lived in common nurseries. As was his custom, Bronson called a family council to talk over the situation. Lizzie and May were too young to understand what was happening, but Anna and Louisa were terribly unhappy at the thought that the family might be split up. They felt their world was about to be torn apart and clung to each other, crying in the night. "I prayed to God to keep us all together," Louisa wrote in her journal.

Eventually Bronson did choose to keep the family together. Mr. Lane and William left soon after, and the Alcotts huddled together in the cold, drafty house that was no longer theirs. Where could they go next? As he so often did, Abba's brother Uncle Samuel came to the rescue. With his help, they were able to rent a house in the nearby town of Still River that was called "Brick Ends" because it was made of wood with brick walls at either end. During the five months that the Alcotts lived in Still River, Anna and Louisa attended Miss Maria Chase's school. Here they found playmates with whom

Did you know...

In the plays young Louisa wrote for her sisters and herself to act out, she always chose the most colorful roles for herself—especially those of villains, pirates, bandits and sword-waving heroes.

they had hoop-rolling contests and acted out plays that Louisa wrote and produced.

On November 14, 1844, two weeks before Louisa's twelfth birthday, the Alcotts moved again. (When she was twenty-eight, Louisa added up the number of times they family had moved so far in her life and found it was twenty-nine.) They were going back to Concord, where they roomed with the Hosmers while they searched for a house. In the spring, they purchased "Hillside" a farmhouse on the Lexington Road near Emerson's home with $1,000 dollars from Abba's father's estate and $500 from Emerson. (After the Alcotts left the house, the author Nathaniel Hawthorne would purchase it and rename it "Wayside.") Many years later Louisa would use her memories of this home in describing the March home in *Little Women*.

The history of the place stirred Louisa's vivid imagination. Paul Revere had galloped down the road in front of the house, and British redcoat soldiers had marched over the pine-covered hill behind it to take part in the opening battle of the Revolutionary War. There was lots of space for running and a big barn that was perfect for performing plays. But one thing bothered her: there were too many people in the house. Mr. Lane and another teacher came to stay with them, and the lack of privacy often made her feel cross. She shared an upstairs bedroom with her sisters, and dreamed of having a room of her own. In a note to her mother, she wrote, "I have tryed to be more contented and I think I have been more so. I have been thinking about my little room which I suppose I shall never have. I should want to be there all the time and I should go there and sing and think."

Louisa's wish for her own room was granted the following year when her father had an old shed on the property divided into two rooms, which were then attached to each end of the house. One of these small wings became a little room for Louisa. In a journal entry in March of 1846 she wrote, "I have at last got the little room I have wanted so long, and am very happy about it. It does me good to be alone." Abba had put sweet-smelling herbs in the closet and arranged Louisa's desk and sewing basket under a window. Here she could keep her treasures and read and write in peace. It even had a door to the outside, so she could run off into the woods when she felt like it.

In their previous life at Concord, the Alcotts had become friends with Emerson's friend Henry David Thoreau. Thoreau and Bronson admired each other's independent way of thinking and determination to live life the way they believed it should be lived. Thoreau had taken the children on nature hikes around Walden Pond, teaching them the names of birds and flowers and delighting them with nature fantasies, such as the idea that a cobweb was a handkerchief dropped by a fairy. Now they went out to visit Thoreau who was living in a house he had built by Walden Pond. He played his flute for them and told them Indian legends about the blue bird carrying the sky on its back and the scarlet tanager flying through the green foliage of the forest to ignite the leaves with color. He rowed them around the pond searching for otters' dens and took them to secret glens where the best blueberries grew.

In her own little room at Hillside, Louisa began to write in earnest—turning out poems, stories, sketches and plays at a great rate. The four Alcott sisters performed the romantic, sentimental plays for their friends and neighbors in the great airy barn behind the house. Louisa was the director, stage manager and wardrobe mistress. She was quite talented with her needle and could make elaborate props and costumes out of cardboard and scraps of cloth. The plays, which had titles such as "The Witches' Curse," "A Captive of Castile," and "The Prince and the Peasant," were gathered up by Anna many years later and published in a book.

Living in this fantasy world through constantly writing and reading romantic stories, Louisa found herself acting out her

Thoreau's Walden Pond in 1996. This famous landmark is still popular today as it was when Thoreau and the Alcott children enjoyed its solitude.

own romantic dream. Ralph Waldo Emerson had been a friend and savior to her family for as long as she could remember. Observing how much she liked to read, he invited her to come and read in his library as often as she liked. Among the stories she read was one about the little girl Bettine who adored the great German poet Goethe. Louisa decided she would be like Bettine. Slipping out of her room at night she climbed into her favorite cherry tree where she sat gazing at the stars and thinking romantic thoughts until swooping owls frightened her back to her bed. She wrote letters to Emerson but never delivered them. As Bettine did for Goethe, Louisa sang a serenade under her hero's window one night, but she sang it in German in a small voice that nobody heard. She also left flowers on his doorstep when nobody was around. Years later when Louisa told Emerson of her teenage crush on him, they laughed about it together, and he asked to see the letters. Unfortunately, they were no longer available—an older and wiser Louisa had burned them.

An illustration by May Alcott for one of Louisa's plays titled "The Bandit's Bride," one of many that she would write and perform along with her sisters for their amusement.

Breadwinner

"I will make a battering-ram of my head and make my way through this rough-and-tumble world."

—Louisa May Alcott

SOMETIME IN HER early teens, Louisa had a deep religious experience. Early one morning while the grass was still covered with dew, she left Hillside for a run. "The moss was like velvet, and as I ran under the arches of yellow and red leaves I sang for joy, my heart was so bright and the world so beautiful," she recalled. A strange and solemn feeling came over her as she watched the sun rise over the river, over the hill and spread across the meadows. Only the rustling of the pines broke the stillness. It seemed, she wrote, "that I *felt* God as I never did before, and I prayed in my heart that I might keep that happy sense of nearness in my life." Towards the end of her life she wrote a note beside this journal entry saying, "I have, for I most sincerely think that the little girl 'got religion' that day in the wood when dear Mother Nature led her to God."

Many parents in the 1840s expected their children to behave like miniature adults. But although Bronson and Abba constantly watched over and directed their girls' moral and spiritual development, they seldom restrained their imaginative fun and games. One day Emerson brought the famous transcendentalist Margaret Fuller to visit. Miss Fuller, who was well known as an educator herself, expressed interest in Bronson's theories of education. As they were standing on the front steps she said she was eager to meet his "model" children.

Just at that moment, a wild uproar was heard. Around the corner of the house came baby May wearing a queen's crown and seated in a wheelbarrow for a carriage. Anna was driving the carriage which was pulled by Louisa, who was the horse, bitted and bridled. Lizzie played the dog, barking as loudly as she could. When they saw the group of adults on the steps, the procession came to a halt. Then Louisa tripped and they all collapsed in a shrieking, laughing heap. Abba waved her hand dramatically and declared, "Here are the model children, Miss Fuller." Many years later Louisa used this incident in her book *An Old-Fashioned Girl*.

In addition to providing a fine venue for performing plays, the barn hosted many other activities. The Pickwick Club (named after Dickens' famous club of the same name) met there. The only members were the

Alcott sisters, and their most important project was to publish a newspaper filled with sentimental stories by Anna, lively poems by Louisa, and simple tales by Lizzie and May.

The girls also had a post office on the hill where they exchanged letters, books, and flowers among themselves and with friends. The post office lasted as long as they lived at Hillside. Eventually Louisa made use of these memories—plays, the Pickwick Club, and the post office—in *Little Women*.

Although Louisa was growing into an attractive young woman with rich chestnut hair, dark eyes and regular features, her long arms and legs occasionally made her feel clumsy and awkward. Like Jo, she frequently wished she were a boy. She had periods of moodiness but was usually cheerful and took the lead in thinking up adventures. Her mischievous spirit sometimes shocked the more proper Anna. One day as they were on their way to school with a friend named Clara, they passed a horse and sleigh standing in front of a neighbor's house. On an impulse, Louisa jumped into the driver's seat. Clara climbed in after her and away they went. Anna watched in dismay as they raced up the street and down again. Then Louisa returned the sleigh, the two climbed out, and they all went on their way to school.

All of the girls learned early in life to do fine sewing. At twelve, Louisa had gone into business as a dolls' dressmaker, hanging out her sign and putting display models in her window. The neighborhood children hired her to sew for their dolls. Her fashionable turbans were especially popular—except with the neighbor's hens, which didn't appreciate being chased down and having their feathers plucked to decorate the dolls' headgear.

At sixteen years of age, Louisa felt more than ever the

need to help with the family income. The Concord schools refused to hire her father because of his reputation for teaching in an unconventional way—and he refused to do any other kind of work for regular wages. Money was a subject he simply didn't discuss. Abba was left to figure out how to feed and clothe the family, and the older girls realized how unhappy it made her to have to continually beg family members and friends for financial help.

It was their good friend Ralph Waldo Emerson who suggested a way for Louisa to help out her family. Why didn't she start a summer school in the barn? He would send his children, and he thought others might also. So she did. As it turned out, however, there were never many pupils, and Louisa found that she really didn't like teaching, although she did it well and energetically. Her favorite student was little Ellen Emerson, who adored her teacher. Ellen often visited Hillside, and Louisa began to weave stories about flowers and birds and fairies for her. Her inspiration for the stories came from her own reading and from tales Thoreau had told her. Nine-year-old Ellen was enchanted with the stories, and at her insistence Louisa wrote them down and gave her copies of them in handmade books. Then she put them away among the romantic plays she had composed. Several years would pass before she thought of them again.

As the winter of 1848 approached, it became clear something had to be done. The family's debts were piling up; their rambling old house needed repairs; and there was little or no prospect for a better income in Concord. Abba Alcott's talent for helping needy people was well known among her friends, and now a group of women in Boston called the South End Friendly Society offered her work. Her job would be to visit poor people and decide how money and goods from various charities should be distributed. Reluctantly, it was decided the family must move back to Boston.

At first they lived in dingy rooms on Dedham Street where Louisa felt like a "caged sea gull." She longed for the "fine, free times" among the hills and woods of Concord. Abba worked hard for a very small salary. Bronson was holding "conversations" at which people paid a small admission to hear him talk about his ideas. May went to school and Lizzie was the housekeeper. Anna and Louisa took whatever jobs they could find. Sometimes they took jobs as babysitters and sometimes they taught a few children. Both were good seamstresses, and they earned money by sewing for other people.

For amusement they made up plays and acted out all the parts. Anna and Louisa made elaborate stage settings and props—including castles and waterfalls, harps and weapons—as well as fancy costumes out of what they could find in the scrap bag. Louisa's plays were filled with romance, excitement and adventure. Anna, who had a real talent for acting, played the leading ladies, and Louisa took all the male roles, stomping across the stage waving a sword and saving fair maidens, who were usually played by Anna.

During her teenage years, Louisa wrote lots of poems and short stories in addition to plays. Only recently it has been discovered that she wrote her first novel, titled *The Inheritance*, at seventeen. It's unknown whether she tried to get the book published during her lifetime. Two researchers, who were looking through her papers at Harvard University, discovered the handwritten manuscript by accident, and it was published by Dutton Books in 1997. Like the plays she was writing at this time, the book is melodramatic and romantic. It tells the story of

Louisa and her sisters would not only put on plays but also design the props and costumes themselves. Pictured here are costumes used in dramas in the 1800's.

Edith, a poor orphan, whose beauty and goodness help her overcome the evil plots of the wicked Lady Ida, and win the love of the handsome Lord Percy.

In her journal, Louisa analyzed her life and "the wilful, moody girl I try to manage." She wrote, "If I look in my glass, I try to keep down vanity about my long hair, my well-shaped head, and my good nose. In the street I try not to covet fine things. My quick tongue is always getting me into trouble, and my moodiness makes it hard to be cheerful when I think how poor we are, how much worry it is to live, and how many things I long to do I never can."

During the next six years, the Alcotts lived in Boston,

moving around to several different houses, sometimes renting rooms and sometimes staying in the home of their generous Uncle Samuel. Abba worked hard, doing a great deal above and beyond her poorly-paid duties as a social worker. She collected bundles of supplies and clothing for the poor, ran a kind of employment agency for women, collected money from anyone she could badger into giving to the needy, and sometimes fed the hungry out of her own slender means. "Our poor little home had much love and happiness in it," Louisa wrote in her journal, "and was a shelter for lost girls, abused wives, friendless children, and weak or wicked men."

One day in the summer of 1850, some poor immigrants came to the gate, and Abba let them into the garden and fed them. It turned out they had smallpox, and soon everyone in the Alcott family came down with it. The girls had slight cases while Abba's was somewhat worse. Bronson, who got the worst case, was so sick he couldn't leave the house for two months. Smallpox was a highly contagious and much-dreaded disease, and with no help from neighbors or doctors, Anna and Louisa nursed their parents back to health themselves.

Louisa was willing to try any kind of honest work that would help her family, whom she described as "poor as rats." One day a gentleman came to the house to ask Abba if she knew of a needy woman who would like to be a companion to his invalid sister, Miss Eliza. He just needed someone to read to her, keep her company and do a little light housekeeping, he explained. Overhearing the conversation, Louisa enthusiastically volunteered to take the position herself. After some hesitation, Abba agreed to let her take it for a month's trial. Wages were not discussed, but the gentleman assured them she would be adequately compensated for her time.

Poor Louisa soon realized she had been tricked. Never was she asked to read to Miss Eliza. Instead, she was expected to perform all of the menial tasks that the lowest-ranked servant would do. Her days were spent carrying great buckets of coal in from the shed and lugging heavy pails of water from the well up steep stairs. She split logs for kindling, took care of the fireplaces, shoveled snow from the walks, and in her spare time cleaned and scrubbed. She was furious but determined to stick out the month to earn money for the family. The one light moment came when the gentleman asked her to black his boots. She flatly refused and later was pleased to see him angrily blacking them himself.

When the month was over and she announced she was leaving, Miss Eliza cried so pitifully Louisa agreed to stay on until a replacement arrived. Two applicants came, took a look at the situation, called Louisa a fool, and left. When the third one arrived, Louisa was ready. She snatched up her packed bag and quickly said goodbye. At the last minute Miss Eliza pressed a little purse into her hand. After seven weeks of servitude Louisa couldn't wait to see what she had earned. As she waited for the bus that would take her home, she eagerly opened the purse—and found in it a mere four dollars! It was a bitter moment, and her outraged family agreed that she should send the insulting sum back. This painful experience she later used in a story called, "How I Went Out to Service" and in a book called *Work*.

The family felt optimistic when Bronson set out for the Midwest to give a series of lectures with eighteen dollars borrowed from Emerson. They optimistically expected that this would be a turning point in their fortunes. When he returned home late one night in February, Abba and the girls rushed downstairs in their white nightgowns to greet him. After he had eaten and recounted his adventures, May finally asked, "Well, did they pay you?" Bronson sadly opened his pocketbook and showed them a one-dollar bill. "Only that," he said, explaining that his overcoat had been stolen and he had to buy a shawl; promises made to him were not kept; and traveling was more expensive that he expected. "But I have opened the way," he said, "and another year shall do better."

Abba, who had counted so much on the success of this trip, kissed him and said, "I call that doing *very well*. Since you are safely home, dear, we don't ask anything more."

Anna and Louisa had to choke back their tears at this display of undying devotion, Louisa recalled, and they "took a little lesson in real love that we never forgot."

There were few job opportunities for respectable women in the 1850s, but Anna and Louisa made the most of their talents for sewing and teaching. Louisa sewed as many as a dozen sheets a day and helped Anna with schools that they taught at different places in Boston, including their own parlor. Correcting slates and listening to endless recitations of the alphabet were not very exciting activities for Louisa, so she kept writing and hoping her pen would earn some money.

Her first published effort was a poem called "Sunlight,"

> ### Did you know...
>
> The Alcotts were followers of Sylvester Graham (creator of the graham cracker) who was famous for his ideas about health. Graham believed in taking cold baths, sleeping on hard mattresses, getting lots of fresh air and always being happy at mealtimes. He was against eating sugar, meat and butter and drinking coffee and tea.

which she published under the name Flora Fairfield, and it appeared in a popular women's magazine called *Peterson's*. Encouraged, Louisa began to work harder at her writing and began to send it to more editors. When a prominent editor advised her in a kindly way to stick to teaching as she was not a writer, she was not discouraged— instead, she took his advice as a challenge. *She* knew she could write. When the *Saturday Evening Gazette*, a national weekly magazine, bought a story and paid her ten dollars, she felt her career was launched. This tale, "The Rival Prima Donnas," is set in a theater and features many characteristics that her early stories share, including sensational scenes involving love and treachery.

On Christmas Day of 1854, Louisa tucked a small red clothbound book into her mother's stocking with a note reading, "Into your Christmas stocking I have put my 'first born,' knowing that you will accept it with all its faults (for grandmothers are always kind)." It was a copy of *Flower Fables*, a collection of the little tales she had written at the age of sixteen for Ellen Emerson. Louisa received thirty-two dollars for the book, which was published in a first edition of 1600 copies and sold well. But the most important thing for Louisa was seeing her name on the title page.

In June of 1855, Cousin Lizzie Wells invited Louisa to spend the summer in Walpole, New Hampshire. It was a wonderful change for the nature-loving young woman. "So glad to run and skip in the woods and up the splendid ravine," she wrote in her journal. "Helped cousin L. in her garden; and the smell of the fresh earth and the touch of the green leaves did me good." In July, the rest of the family came to live rent-free in a friend's house in Walpole. "Plays, picnics, pleasant people, and good neighbors," Louisa noted.

During the summer and fall in Walpole, Louisa had worked on another book of flower tales and fables, but it was finished too late for the Christmas market, and she could not sell it. Facing the hard fact that her writing could not yet support the family, she decided to return to Boston alone—where she could earn money teaching and sewing while she wrote more of the romantic stories that magazines were willing to buy.

In November of 1855, Louisa took the stagecoach to Boston, carrying with her a small trunk of clothes she had made herself, twenty dollars from her writing earnings, and a stack of manuscripts she hoped to sell. It was the first time she had been entirely on her own, and she was determined to succeed. "Won't go home to sit idle while I have a head and pair of hands," she promised herself.

Mr. and Mrs. Alcott with Louisa and Anna pushing her son Frederick in front of Orchard House, which Louisa called "Apple Slump" due to its need of constant repairs.

5

Nurse

"Though often home sick, heart sick & worn out, I like it . . . ."
—Louisa May Alcott

ON NOVEMBER 29, 1855—their joint birthday—twenty-three-year old Louisa wrote an affectionate letter to her fifty-six year old father, telling him she had no gift to offer but "a heart full of love." She said she wished that he could teach her so that "at fifty-six I may be as young at heart and full of cheerful courage as this day finds you." What she didn't say was that his cheerful refusal to work at anything that didn't suit his lofty ideas had driven her to assume the burden of supporting the family at such an early age.

And work she did that winter and spring. In Boston, her cousins, the Sewalls, gave her a place to stay while she sewed, taught, and wrote. One of her tasks was to sew a set of shirts for the pastor of the Federal Street Church. She also acted as governess to the children of the Lovering family. And she worked away at her stories— sensational thrillers that popular magazines bought for fifteen or twenty dollars apiece.

In June she rejoined the family in Walpole where she found Lizzie very ill from scarlet fever, contracted from some poor children Abba had nursed. The children had been living over a cellar where pigs had been kept. Their landlord, a church deacon, refused to clean the place until Abba threatened to sue him. By that time two of the children had died and May and Lizzie had come down with the disease. May recovered quickly, but Lizzie's condition was precarious. Through the summer Louisa nursed her sister, did housework and wrote a story a month. When fall came Lizzie was still weak, but Louisa felt she must return to Boston where she could earn more money for the family. It was a sad parting. "I don't often pray in words," Louisa wrote, "but when I set out that day...my heart was very full, and I said to the Lord, 'Help us all, and keep us for one another.'"

She settled in a boarding house in Boston in an attic room that she called her "sky parlor" like the one where Jo March lived and wrote in New York in *Little Women*. Cousin Lizzie Wells gave her tickets to a course of lectures, a new cloak, and an elegant black silk dress. Other relatives took her to the theater, and her father's friends, Dr. and Mrs. Theodore Parker, often invited her into their home. Louisa had great admiration for

Dr. Parker, a Unitarian minister, who attracted large crowds that came to hear him denounce slavery. She especially liked his courage in acting on his beliefs. He was known to have hidden a runaway slave in his house on one occasion and to have married two runaway slaves on another. His warm friendship and encouragement heartened the lonely young woman, who said, "He is like a great fire, where all can come and be warmed and comforted!"

In the spring Louisa returned to Walpole, satisfied with her winter's accomplishments, which she recorded as a list: ". . . supported myself, written eight stories, taught four months, earned a hundred dollars, and sent money home." Anna was home from her teaching job in Syracuse, and the family was happy to be together. However, they were all anxious about Lizzie, who had never recovered her health after having scarlet fever. Lizzie's welfare became the chief concern of the family for the next year as she gradually became weaker.

It was decided that a return to peaceful Concord, with its pleasant associations and old friends, might help Lizzie gain strength. With Emerson's assistance, the Alcotts bought Orchard House, a dilapidated old farmhouse. While it was being repaired they moved into temporary rooms in Concord. As the new year of 1858 began, Lizzie was much worse, and the doctor told the family nothing more could be done for her. Anna took over the housekeeping so Abba and Louisa could devote themselves to taking care of the invalid. "Sad, quiet days in her room, and strange nights keeping up the fire and watching the dear shadow try to while away the long, sleepless nights without troubling me," Louisa wrote. When Lizzie gave up the struggle and died early in March, Louisa said, "I am glad to know she is safe from pain and age in some world where her innocent soul must by happy."

Louisa's bedroom at Orchard House. The desk was built by Bronson Alcott for Louisa and her writing.

Ten years later in *Little Women*, Louisa recreated her patient, loving sister in the character of Beth and revealed the depth of her grief in the feelings of Jo, her own duplicate self.

When Anna announced her engagement in April to John Pratt, the son of a Concord family, Louisa was dismayed. John, who worked as a clerk, was a kind, dependable man, but the prospect of losing another sister was painful. Death and love, Louisa felt, were disrupting the close family life that mattered so much to her. As usual, work was the best remedy for her distress, and she spent the summer helping the family make their new home, Orchard House, livable. She was never fond of the house, which needed constant repairs, and called it "Apple Slump."

Louisa returned to Boston in October to seek employment. At first it was not easy to find. In her depressed state, she took a walk along the Mill Dam which created the Back Bay. Looking at the sluggish water, she was tempted to end her troubles by jumping into it. But she thought of her family who still needed her, and her courage returned. "It seemed cowardly to run away before the battle was over," she said. She found work again as a governess to the Lovering family, and in her spare time wrote stories. Most of them were still the kind of story she called "rubbish," but the money they earned paid the family bills. "Someday," she wrote in her journal, "I'll do my best, and get paid for it."

That day came sooner than she expected when her short story "Love and Self Love" appeared in the March 1860 issue of the highly-respected *Atlantic Monthly Magazine*. With the payment of fifty dollars she bought a carpet, rejoicing that "wild Louisa's head" could keep the feet of the family warm. When the *Atlantic* bought a second story ("A Modern Cinderella" based on the love story of Anna and John) and paid her seventy-five dollars for it, she felt that after ten years of hard climbing, she had finally found a "perch" on the ladder to success.

On May 23, 1860, Anna and John Pratt were married by Uncle Samuel at Orchard House in a simple wedding. The bride wore a silver-gray silk dress with lilies of the valley in her hair. There was dancing and a little wedding feast provided by their neighbors, and then the couple left amid a rain of kisses and tears. Louisa recorded that the house was "filled with sunshine, flowers, friends, and happiness." But, she added, "I mourn the loss of my Nan, and am not comforted." Meg's wedding in *Little Women* is almost identical, and Jo's feelings are the same as Louisa's. Happily, Louisa and Jo soon came to see Anna's John and Meg's John as wonderful additions to their families.

Although her stories and books are filled with love and marriage, Louisa chose to remain single. She quickly discouraged several men who tried to court her. One of them wrote her love letters and "haunted" the road in front of her house. Victorian women frequently married to help their families financially, so when a fairly wealthy man proposed, Louisa asked her mother's advice. After Abba found that Louisa didn't love the man, she advised her not to marry him. Louisa realized that even in a love match, a woman in the nineteenth century lost her identity when she married and had few rights of her own. Having observed how difficult married life was for her mother and how soon Anna became submerged in domesticity no doubt influenced her own decision to remain independent. After visiting Anna in her "sweet and pretty" little home, she noted that it suited her sister, but added, "I'd rather be a free spinster and paddle my own canoe."

Concord, which had denied Bronson Alcott a job as a teacher in its schools, relented and made him superintendent of schools in 1860. Although the salary was small, he enjoyed the position and the chance to have some of his teaching theories put into practice. One of his innovations was to have a festival to celebrate the end of the school year. Louisa wrote a "Children's Song" for the 1860 festival and was thrilled to hear four hundred little voices singing her song. It became popular with the children, and seventy of them surprised Louisa and her father by parading to their house to serenade them with it. Bronson dashed down to the cellar to return with a basket of apples to pass out among the children and then led them in a dance, "hoppity skipping" until they were exhausted.

In January of 1861, Louisa was working on a book based on her own experiences called *Work*. But when her mother became ill, she "corked up" her inkstand and nursed her back to health. In May, she became a nurse again when her cousin Lizzie fell ill. Louisa realized she was good at taking care of sick people, and she began to wonder if she should take up nursing as her career.

The Alcotts had long been staunch abolitionists, and when the radical abolitionist John Brown had come to speak and raise money at a Town Hall meeting in Concord, Louisa had been in the audience. She was fired up by his speech and agreed with his argument that the only answer to slavery was war. Brown's futile raid on Harper's Ferry inspired her to write, "Glad I have lived to see the Antislavery movement and this last heroic act in it. Wish I could do my part in it." After Brown was captured, condemned and hung, Concord held a memorial service in the Town Hall on December 2, 1859. Bronson Alcott, Emerson, and Thoreau all took part in the service, and Louisa contributed a poem with a verse saying

> No monument of quarried stone,
> No eloquence of speech,
> Can grave the lessons on the land
> His martyrdom will teach . . . .

On April 15, 1861, Fort Sumter was fired on and the Civil War began. Most people believed it would be over in a few months, slavery would end, and the country would be united again. "In Concord," Louisa told a friend, "everyone is boiling over with excitement..." On April 19, Louisa, along with most of the villagers, went to see Concord's volunteer soldiers leave on the train amid great fanfare, including band music, singing, speeches and flag waving. She wished she could go with them. Sewing blue flannel shirts and picking lint from cotton bolls for bandages did not satisfy her lust for action.

Louisa's dear friend and teacher Henry David Thoreau died from tuberculosis in May. At his memorial service, Bronson read from Thoreau's writings, and Louisa felt that Thoreau's own "wise and pious thoughts" proved him a better Christian than those who condemned him for not attending church services. His life was too short, Louisa wrote to a friend, but she felt sure it would continue to "blossom and grow" after his death. Later that year she wrote a poem honoring her friend. Called "Thoreau's Flute," it was published in the *Atlantic Monthly Magazine* in September 1863.

By the fall of 1862 the war news was grim. During the first year of fighting, most of the important battles had been won by the South, and the numbers of sick and wounded were piling up in hospitals. Louisa had proved a good nurse in taking care of her relatives, and although she had no formal training, neither did most of the women who were volunteering as nurses. Florence Nightingale had established the first school of nursing in London in 1860, but the United States would not have nursing schools until 1873. Fortunately, a capable Superintendent of Women Nurses named Dorothea Dix had been appointed to recruit and oversee the work of nurses during the Civil War.

Did you know...

Louisa never forgot the sight of wounded and dying men arriving at the Union Hotel Hospital in Washington after the Battle of Fredericksburg where 17,900 men died on the battlefield.

As the hospitals became more crowded, Miss Dix sent out a call for nursing volunteers "between thirty-five and fifty, strong, matronly, sober, industrious, and neat." Louisa met all the requirements except the age bracket. She was only thirty, but upon the strong recommendations of well-known friends, she was accepted.

Her sister May and her friend Julian Hawthorne saw her off on the Concord train, and after spending the night in Boston with Anna and John, she made her way to Washington by way of train, boat, and horse car. She was assigned to the Union Hotel Hospital where she found herself surrounded by three or four hundred men in all stages of suffering, disease, and dying. The building itself she described as a "perfect pestilence-box": cold, damp, dirty, and full of vile odors from wounds, kitchens, washrooms, and stables.

She got up at six, dressed by gaslight and ran through her ward flinging up the windows to get rid of the stale air, although the men shivered and grumbled. She joked and coaxed, poked up the fire and added blankets to their beds. Breakfast was fried beef, coarse bread and weak coffee. Back on her ward, she passed out rations, feeding the men who couldn't feed themselves, dressed wounds, carried out the doctors' orders, trained her aides in making beds or sweeping floors, and "rushed up and down after pillows, linens, and sponges." After the men ate their noon meal, she wrote letters that they dictated until it was time to serve the five o'clock supper. Then the doctors made their last rounds, and the last medicines were handed out. At nine o'clock the bell rang, the gaslight was dimmed, and the weary nurses went to bed.

Shortly after Louisa arrived at the hospital, the Battle of Fredericksburg—one of the bloodiest battles of the Civil War—took place. Huge ambulance wagons drawn by four horses began delivering terribly wounded men to the hospital. It was a cold, rainy December and some of the men had lain in the mud for days, waiting to be transported to the hospitals. Some were so caked with mud it took repeated washings to remove all the grime. Hoping her hearty good will and sympathy would make up for her ignorance, awkwardness, and bashfulness, Louisa set to work to do everything she could to relieve their suffering.

When she could snatch a few minutes from her duties, Louisa recorded her experiences in letters to her family. She told them about individual patients, like the big handsome blacksmith from Virginia who had a severe chest wound and was courageously facing death. He was just her age, and like her, was devoted to his family, for whose sake he had never married. In his helplessness, he came to depend on and confide in her, and she comforted his with all the warmth and compassion she could summon until he died. In her journal, she was making notes of the people she worked with: the "sanctified" nurse who stole from the patients; the doctor who drank so much that his hands shook—so badly, in fact, that he couldn't even operate; the staff members who were unconcerned about their patients and those who cared deeply; the dedicated matron of the hospital who was dying from typhoid fever.

In January, Louisa became ill, suffering "a sharp pain in the side, cough, fever, and dizzyness . . . " She was diagnosed as having "pneumonia typhoid" and ordered to stay in her room. For as long as she could, she wrote letters, sewed for "her boys" and refused to be sent home. But when she became much worse and her mind became confused, her family was notified. One day she woke out of a mixed-up dream to see her father's face looking down at her. For five more days she resisted leaving the hospital, hoping to recover and return to her duties. But finally she felt so ill she agreed to let Bronson take her home.

Several of the staff, as well as a number of her patients who could walk, saw her off. Miss Dix, the nursing super-visor, brought a basket filled with wine, tea, medicine, cologne, a blanket, pillow, fan, and a New Testament for the journey. Louisa arrived home in a delirium imagining that the house had no roof. Shocked by her appearance and condition, Abba and May took turns with Bronson in nursing her. She suffered terrible nightmares and had strange visions. At times she imagined she was being burnt as a witch or that she was taking care of millions of sick men "who never died or got well."

The family tried to keep Anna, who was seven months pregnant, from knowing how sick Louisa was, but Anna insisted on seeing her. She was appalled by Louisa's brownish skin, her bloodshot eyes with great hollows under them, her swollen tongue, uncontrollable cough, and her demented stare.

Louisa had been liberally treated with calomel, a mercury compound. It was a favorite medicine with many doctors in the nineteenth century and had gained a bad reputation for being overused. A popular poem about calomel (which consisted of about twelve verses and existed in many versions) asked this question about doctors:

> How many patients have they lost
> How many thousands they make ill
> Of poison, with their *Calomel*?

She had the symptoms of mercury poisoning, and although she stopped having delusions after three weeks and slowly regained her strength, she never recovered the robust health she had enjoyed before her hospital experience. Her beautiful hair, a yard and a half in length, was all cut off, and she wore lace caps to cover her baldness. She felt sad at losing her "one beauty." But, never mind, she wrote in her journal, "a wig outside is better than a loss of wits inside."

Louisa's writing career was starting to become successful, and she used the money earned from her stories to help her family in repairing Orchard House.

Celebrity

"People begin to come and stare at the Alcotts. Reporters haunt the place to look at the authoress, who dodges into the woods . . . and won't be even a very small lion."

—Louisa May Alcott

ON MARCH 28, 1863, Bronson came rushing home from Boston to announce that Anna and John had "a fine boy." Abba cried, May laughed, and Louisa said, "I *knew* it wouldn't be a girl!" With the coming of spring Louisa felt "born again;" everything seemed beautiful and new. She enjoyed drives and little walks and set to work sewing shirts and gowns for her "blessed nephew." When she visited him in Boston later that month, she found him "ugly but promising."

There was also another piece of good news. A story of hers, "Pauline's Passion and Punishment," won a hundred-dollar prize in a contest. It was one of her "thriller" stories, and although she told a friend it wasn't worth reprinting, the money was most welcome. The periodical in which it was published, *Frank Leslie's Illustrated Newspaper*, specialized in murders, bizarre crimes, and gory catastrophes. Louisa instructed Leslie to publish her story under the pen name A. M. Barnard. And for the next five years she wrote sensational stories under that name for *Leslie's* and other similar periodicals.

Bronson had shown Frank Sanborn, the editor of the Boston abolitionist paper *The Commonwealth*, extracts from the letters Louisa had written home, describing her experiences in the Union Hospital in Washington. As soon as she was able to do a little work again, Sanborn urged her to arrange them for publication. Needing money as always for family debts, she agreed. Calling herself Nurse Periwinkle, she described the tragedies and the heroism she had witnessed, the patience and fortitude of the most seriously wounded, the jokes and funny happenings that made the days endurable. She told the stories of "her boys": John Sulie, the big, brave mortally-wounded blacksmith; Sergeant Bain, who wrote love letters to his sweetheart with his left hand because his right arm was disabled; the cheerful Irishman who called her "darlin," blessed her for her care, and wished her an "aisy bed above"; and Billy, the twelve-year-old drummer boy, who mourned for his friend, Kit, who had carried him from the battlefield to safety and then dropped dead from his wounds.

The sketches, which were published in four installments in May and June of 1863 in the *The Commonwealth,* were received with an enthusiasm that overwhelmed Louisa.

People were hungry for war news and eager to know what might happen to their fighting sons, brothers, fathers, husbands, and sweethearts if they were sent to hospitals. Her simple, frank retelling of life in the hospital satisfied a need to know, and copies of the paper sold so quickly the publisher couldn't print them fast enough to meet the demand.

Requests poured in for more of the same, and Louisa agreed to enlarge the sketches and have them published as a book. *Hospital Sketches* appeared in August and received high praise from critics and friends for its vivid writing. Although the small volume never made much money for its author, its success convinced her that this true-to-life, direct kind of writing was her best style. Eventually, developing that style would lead her to write the novels that brought fame and fortune. But that happy eventuality was still several books, stories, and years away.

As the war ground on with ever-greater casualty lists, Louisa hoped she would recover her strength and be able to return to nursing, but she was still very weak and not capable of any strenuous physical activity. She slept badly and tired easily, but she poured what energy she had into her writing. Her stories paid for a new roof and other repairs to Orchard House, which she referred to as the "sinking fund" as it swallowed up money as fast as she earned it.

Hoping to make more than the pittance she was paid for her stories, she pulled out the manuscripts of two novels she had begun before the Civil War. When she showed *Moods* to a publisher, he told her it was too long. After she had shortened and rearranged the material, it was accepted and published. On Christmas Eve of 1864, she received ten copies of the book. It received mixed reviews, and she was never as pleased with the shortened version as she had been with the original. Sylvia, the heroine of the book, is like Louisa, a young woman dominated by her moods, while the hero, Adam, is like Thoreau. Adam's profession is "studying the world," and his physical description fits Louisa's vision of her beloved friend. Adam is tall and broad-shouldered, bronzed by wind and weather with a "massive head covered with rings of ruddy brown hair, gray eyes, imminent nose" and a face stamped with "power, intellect, and courage." She used her "*Moods* money" to pay off family debts.

In April, Louisa went to Boston to visit the Pratts. She was there to see the grand celebrations when Richmond, Virginia—the capital of the Confederacy—fell to Union forces, and she was there to witness the mourning when news arrived of the assassination of President Lincoln. She had especially admired him for making plans for the education of former slaves, and she was pleased to observe that in a public procession, a black man and a white man marched arm in arm.

That spring people realized that the long war was finally over and that they could think of other things than battles and death and injuries. It was even possible to travel again. Louisa had long dreamed of seeing Europe, and now an unexpected opportunity opened. William Weld, a Boston shipping merchant who had heard that Louisa was a good nurse, asked her to accompany his daughter Anna and his son George on a tour of Europe. Anna's health was poor, and he wanted her to try the popular water cures at several fashionable spas. For young George, it would be the European grand tour that many wealthy families in the nineteenth century gave their children who were college students in order to complete their educations.

Louisa felt some doubts about the trip, but her relatives and friends all urged her to go, so she agreed to it. On July 20, 1865, they sailed from Boston on the *China*. Although she wasn't actually seasick, Louisa suffered from a queasy feeling during the entire nine-day trip and was happy to set foot on dry land in England. After spending four drizzly days in

London, they left for the continent. In Germany, she found Cologne to be "hot, dirty, and evil-smelling," and she ended up spending their three days there nursing her companions, who were both ill. Louisa found a trip down the Rhine River delightful, but Anna didn't like the boat, so they persuaded the captain to let them off.

Making their way overland, they reached a small town in Bavaria where Anna took the water cure under the care of a doctor. Louisa was bored as well as worried as to how to please her fretful patient. In her journal she noted, "Hers is a very hard case to manage and needs the patience and wisdom of an angel." A letter from home cheered her up; she was touched and pleased at how much they missed her and longed for her return.

As they traveled through Germany, Louisa found that the Welds didn't share her enthusiasm for seeing historical sites and visiting the home of great writers like Goethe, and she felt frustrated at having to curtail her sightseeing. Finally they reached Vevey, a beautiful town on Lake Geneva in Switzerland. Anna and Louisa settled in the Pension Victoria while George went on to Paris. Louisa made careful notes on the other guests and later used many of them in a story called "Life in a Pension."

The one guest whom Anna and Louisa both found most agreeable was an eighteen-year-old Polish man named Ladislas Wisniewski. He told them he had fought in the Polish rebellion against Russia in 1863 and had been imprisoned, consequently losing his health and his fortune. He and Louisa traded French and English lessons. She

Did you know...

Louisa May Alcott published her first story at age 22, and during the next 34 years until her death at age 56, she published over 30 books, and collections of short stories.

called him "Laddie" and he called her a Polish word meaning "Little Mamma." He was lively and witty and brightened up their days, planning walking and sailing trips and playing music for them. When it was time for Anna and Louisa to leave for Nice, France, he went with them as far as Lausanne where he kissed their hands and bid them a sad farewell, promising they would meet again.

Although they had comfortable rooms in Nice, and Louisa could enjoy drives with Anna and sometimes escape for a walk by herself, she still found the life tiresome. Her patient was increasingly hard to please, and she longed to be free. Finally in May, she quit the position that had become wearing on her and left Anna in the care of a companion and maid. Ladislas met her in Paris and took her to her room. Feeling "as happy as a freed bird," she enjoyed two weeks of sightseeing in the French capital with Ladislas. In the evenings she could read, write or do whatever she chose.

Returning to London, she made up for the miserable time she had there at the beginning of the tour, devouring all the sights and sounds of that fascinating city, meeting political and literary figures, and hearing Charles Dickens do a reading. She also visited a London publisher who paid her five pounds (equivalent to twenty-five American dollars) for the right to publish *Moods*, and asked her for another book. She was introduced as Miss Alcott, the American authoress, and was entertained by distinguished people in London and in their country homes.

Louisa sailed for home in July on the *Africa*. After fourteen stormy days of miserable seasickness, she was delighted to reach Boston and see John Pratt waiting on the wharf to meet her. She had been away for a year. The next day in Concord, her family gave her a joyful welcome. Anna was there with her two boys, and they all had a happy reunion.

Louisa was concerned for her mother, who looked old, tired and sick. Her father was as placid as ever, and debts and unpaid bills had accumulated while the moneymaker was away. Fortunately, there was plenty of work for her to do without searching for it. Offers from half a dozen publishers for short stories were waiting, and she began writing as fast as she could. Friends and relatives, eager to see her after her long absence frequently interrupted her work, and caring for her ailing mother took up a good deal of her time, even though she had hired a competent woman to help with the care. Despite these obstacles, she managed to write twelve stories in less than three months.

The winter of 1866 was a hard one. Louisa pushed herself too far and developed a bad cold that she couldn't throw off. She suffered from neuralgia and terrible headaches and felt "nervous and generally used up." Abba had rheumatic fever and problems with her eyes and her father was lame from arthritis. The family continued to be feeble throughout the cold, wet spring, and it was June before Louisa began to write again.

During July and August, she completed more of her fairy tales and poetry for a book called *Morning Glories*. Unpaid bills worried her so much that she wrote in her journal, "I dread debt more than the devil!" Any writing opportunity that paid interested her. When Thomas Niles, a partner in Roberts Brothers Publishing Company, suggested she write a book for girls, she said she would try. And when a publisher asked her to be the editor of a children's magazine called *Merry's Museum*, she said she would try.

She began on the girls' book but wasn't satisfied with it. Telling Mr. Niles that she didn't know much about girls (except for her own sisters) and understood—and liked— boys better, she put that project aside. The editorial job seemed more of a sure thing. It involved reading manuscripts and writing one story and an editorial for each issue, and she agreed to take it for $500 a year. Many distractions kept her from her work in Concord, so she decided to go to

Boston, where she rented a room on the top floor of 6 Hayward Place in downtown Boston, near the offices of *Merry's Museum*. She called it "Gamp's Garret" (after the nurse Sarah Gamp in a novel by Charles Dickens).

Louisa felt happy and satisfied in this hideaway. The winter of 1867-68 was much easier than the preceding one, and Louisa rejoiced that all of the family were better off. Abba and Bronson were comfortable in Concord; Anna was content with her "good John" and babies; May was busy teaching drawing classes; and she herself was spending busy, happy days with freedom and strength to do her work. When her first hyacinth bloomed at New Year's, she thought it was an omen that the "pathetic family" (as she sometimes referred to the Alcotts) was marching with flags flying into a "new world with the new year." She had no idea how right her prophecy would prove to be.

Louisa had not lost her love for the stage, and during the winter and spring, she acted twelve times in plays put on for charities. Since her money was needed for the family, she considered this a way of contributing to the needy whom the charities supported. She also sewed for the family—a flannel housecoat for Abba, a bonnet for May, and shirts for her nephews. As she sat in her sky parlor "spinning yarns like a spider," she was thankful that publishers were now asking for more stories than she could turn out, when before she had "gone begging" to them with her stories.

At the end of February as she regretfully packed to leave her quiet room, Louisa summed up her winter's work: eight long tales, ten short ones, stacks of manuscripts read, and editorials written. Her mother could sit at rest with many comforts without the "hounds of care and debt worrying her, and that," Louisa wrote in her journal, "is better than any amount of fame to me."

In May, Mr. Niles again reminded her that he wanted a "girls' story." The idea must have been simmering in her mind

A still from the 1994 movie adaptation of Little Women *showing the four March girls with their mother Marmee.*

because now she had a plan. She would write about her own family and set the scene in the Hillside house where she had lived her happiest years. She would include their games, the plays they performed in the barn, their jokes, their scrapes, their petty quarrels, and the deep love that bound the family together. Their favorite book, *The Pilgrim's Progress*, would be interwoven into the lives of Meg, Jo, Beth, and Amy just as it was in the lives of Anna, Louisa, Lizzie, and May. Marmee, their dearly beloved mother, would be the heart of the March family just as Abba was the heart of the Alcott family.

Laurie, the boy next door, would be a combination of Ladislas and Alf Whitman, a young blond-haired boy who had boarded with the Pratts while he went to school in Concord. Although he was fifteen to Louisa's twenty-three at the time, they shared a love of acting in the local dramatic company and an addiction to Charles Dickens' works. After Alf left Concord, he and Louisa kept up a lively correspondence, and now she told him she was putting him in the story along with Ladislas as Laurie, explaining that "You are the sober half and my Ladislas . . . is the gay whirligig half."

All day long Louisa wrote at the small writing table under her bedroom window. She became convinced that a simple, lively book for girls was needed, but had doubts about her ability to write it. Her confidence was not helped by the fact that Mr. Niles was not enthusiastic about the early chapters she sent him. By July 15, the book—all 402 pages—was finished. She was extremely tired and suffered painful headaches from overwork.

The page proofs of the book came in August, and Louisa found it read better than she expected. Mr. Niles was also more enthusiastic than he had been over the early chapters. A bachelor, he had wisely shown the manuscript to some young girls who were unanimous in their praise of it and delighted that someone had finally written a book just for them. Roberts Brothers made her an offer for the book, but suggested it would be to her advantage to keep the copyright, so she did. Keeping the copyright meant she would earn money on each copy sold and would have control over the future of the book. Several years later after the book had made her fortune, she wrote in her journal, "An honest publisher and a lucky author."

When the book appeared in September, reviewers complained about the rather crude illustrations May had done for it, but the book itself received high praise. All 2000 copies of the first edition sold in September, and another 4,500 were printed by the end of the year. Letters began to pour in, visitors arrived in overwhelming numbers, and Louisa found herself sought out for autographs.

Mr. Niles was greatly pleased that his doubts had been proven wrong, and he urged her to begin on a second part of the book. But again Louisa had doubts. The little women in the book were now grown, and she wondered if girls would want to read about their lives as wives and mothers. When he showed

A still from the 1994 movie adaptation of Little Women *showing Jo (played by Winona Ryder) with Laurie (played by Christian Bale), whose character was based on two men Louisa knew—Ladislas Wiesniewski and Alf Whitman.*

her stacks of letters begging for more about the sisters and wanting to know about their marriages, she gave in. But she insisted, "I won't marry Jo to Laurie to please anybody."

In October she rented a room on Brookline Street in Boston and started the second part of *Little Women*, writing a chapter a day. On New Year's Day of 1869 she sent a manuscript of part two to Roberts Brothers. She was exhausted but thankful for the success of the book she had written so reluctantly. "Paid up all the debts," she recorded, "every penny that money can pay—and now I feel as if I could die in peace. My dream is beginning to come true and if my head holds out I'll do all I once hoped to do."

Louisa reading Little Women *to children. Its amazing popularity led to Louisa's life changing in many ways, but she was grateful that its success allowed for her family to escape poverty. However, its success was starting to take its toll on her, and she longed for a vacation.*

Traveler

Soon up among the grand old Alps
She found two blessed things,
The health she had so nearly lost,
And rest for weary limbs.

—"The Lay of a Golden Goose"
by Louisa May Alcott

LOUISA FELT TERRIBLE all during the winter and spring of 1869 after the strenuous effort of writing the two parts of *Little Women* with such fierce concentration. Headaches, a nagging cough, and aching limbs made her feel dull and "used up." But as she noted in her journal, she tried to keep going, since the family seemed panic-stricken and helpless when she broke down. So she continued to plod away at her editorial duties for *Merry's Museum*—which had become tiresome—and tried to write short stories.

The second volume of *Little Women* appeared in April, and Louisa's fame increased. Reporters came to interview her, and people stared at her in the street. She was happy that her books were so well-liked, but hated losing her privacy. To escape the pressure and have a rest, she and May went to Mount Desert, an island off the coast of Maine, for a month. Then she spent the month of July with cousins in Canada.

In August, her hospital sketches were reprinted with eight additional stories. This new edition, which was called *Hospital Sketches and Camp and Fireside Stories*, sold 2,000 copies the first week. Money from sales of *Little Women* continued to pour in, and Louisa rejoiced that all debts (going as far back as the time of her father's Temple School) were paid and she had some cash left over. She entrusted her extra money to her Uncle Samuel Sewall, who invested it wisely so that she began to realize an additional income from the interest on the investment. Bronson was also having a little luck for a change. He wrote a book on his philosophies that was well received, and he was attracting more interest in his lectures and even making a little money from them. Never again would the "pathetic" family suffer from poverty.

Success brought increasing demands. Louisa's reading fans and her publisher pleaded for another book. She had been running monthly installments in *Merry's Museum* of a story about an old-fashioned girl named Polly, and now she set to work to turn the serial into a book. She and May took rooms on Pinckney Street in Boston in the fall while their parents went to stay with the Pratts. Louisa was suffering a great deal from the mercury poison in her body. She said that she wrote *An Old-Fashioned Girl* "with left hand in a sling, one foot up, head aching, and no voice." Polly, the heroine of *An Old-Fashioned Girl*, is not based on Louisa in the same way Jo is in *Little Women*, but she suffers many of as the same trials as her creator as she tries to work her way out of poverty and overcome the snobbery of the society of her day.

When the manuscript was finished, Louisa began to think

> **Did you know...**
>
> **Louisa May Alcott is best known for her domestic tales for juvenile readers. Only recently has the amazing variety of her writing been appreciated. She wrote fairy stories and animal tales for very young children; romantic and gothic tales, autobiographical fiction, and poems for adults; and short stories and essays for all ages on a large variety of subjects.**

of a long vacation. May was eager to go to Europe to sketch and study art, and May's friend, Alice Bartlett, who spoke French and Italian, also wanted to go. Excitedly, they began preparing for a year abroad. On April 1, John Pratt escorted the three women by train from Boston to New York. When the trainboy came through and tried to sell Louisa a copy of *An Old-Fashioned Girl* (which had come out in March), she told him she didn't care for it. He protested that it was a "bully book" (meaning a good book) and that he had sold many copies of it. When John told him she had written the book, the boy stared at her with his mouth hanging open.

The twelve-day crossing on the French steamer the *Lafayette* was cold and rainy. Louisa's seasickness subsided after the first two days, but she suffered from dizziness and stayed below in her cabin for most of the trip. They landed on April 14 in Brest, France, and spent six sunny, happy weeks in the ancient town of Dinan. Alice proved to be a most congenial traveling companion, and the three women reveled in their funny mishaps, amazement at strange customs, and delight in the picturesque architecture of the quaint town. Their letters home described their adventures in exploring ruined castles, being chased by angry pigs, riding in a donkey cart with a tipsy driver, and eating the fresh local foods until they were "fat and hearty."

The only drawback to Louisa's contentment was her health. Her legs pained her so much she couldn't sleep, and her headaches never stopped. When she heard of an excellent English doctor named Dr. Kane in the area, she consulted him. He blamed her problems on the calomel she had been given for her typhoid fever, and told her he suffered the same symptoms because of being overdosed with calomel when he had jungle fever in India. The mercury stays in the body, he explained, until a weak spot occurs, and then goes there to make trouble. He recommended she take wine to help her circulation, wear long woolen underwear to keep warm, and drink iodine of potash as an antidote. Whether this treatment actually worked or not, the pain in her leg eased up, she slept better, and was again able to enjoy her surroundings. She wrote to John Pratt, who had also been treated with large doses of calomel and was now ill and lame, recommending the treatment to him.

As summer arrived, the travelers moved on to Geneva.

This time Louisa could linger and look at monuments and landscapes and ancient castles without a fretful invalid making her hurry past scenes she wanted to explore. Soon after they reached Switzerland, the Franco-Prussian War broke out. France's Emperor Napoleon III was making his last stand, dreaming of restoring the glory days of his uncle, the legendary Napoleon Bonaparte. Their hotel on Lake Geneva was full of refugees, and the three Americans listened to and observed with great interest the excitement of these people who were involved in history-making changes taking place in Europe.

From America, editors kept bombarding Louisa with requests to write for their papers or magazines. In August she wrote to Mr. Niles, telling him she had no intention of getting back on the "treadmill" until her year's vacation was over. However, she enclosed a poem called "The Lay of a Golden Goose," which she told him he could print to appease her petitioners. The poem, in thirty-one four-line stanzas, traces her development as a writer from the time she was "a little goose" who was laughed at for trying to use her wings to fly and advised to stay in her own "puddle." It goes on through her failures and determination until she comes to a stream ("most fertile of all Niles") where suddenly a cry is heard that "This goose lays golden eggs." The goose is then stuffed with praise and requests until she runs to the "Atlantic pond" and paddles across it for her life. The last stanza says that when the "prayers for letters, tales, or verse" pursued her across the ocean, the rejuvenated fowl "Took from her wing a quill and wrote/This lay of a Golden Goose." The poem, which cleverly sums up her career, appeared in several publications.

In October, the travelers enjoyed a memorable journey to Italy, traveling over the Alps by moonlight. After a few "heavenly days" at the lakes, they visited the cities of Milan, Parma, Pisa, Bologna, and Florence. The lovely scenery, Louisa thought, made up for "faded pictures, chilly art galleries, and cold winds in sunny Italy." In Rome, they settled into a warm and cozy apartment on the Piazza Barbarini for the winter. Luckily, their apartment was up high, and they stayed dry when heavy rains caused the Tiber River to over-flow its banks and flood the city.

December brought the sad news of the death of John Pratt. He was just thirty-seven, and from his symptoms it has been speculated that it was mercury poisoning that caused his death. Louisa wrote her sister a loving letter, telling her that, "no born brother was ever dearer, and each year I loved and respected and admired him more and more." John Pratt had been a strong support to Abba during the ten years of his marriage to Anna, and Louisa was anxious about her mother. Cousin Lizzie had asked Abba to come to stay with her for a while, and Louisa wrote to thank her for her kindness to Anna and Abba. She asked Lizzie to fill her place until she could come home. She longed to be with the family, but as she told her cousin, "winter, distance, health and duty hold me till April."

What she could do was try to fulfill the promise she had made to John Pratt to help take care of his children if anything happened to him. And she set about doing it in the only way she could think of—writing a book. And so she began to write *Little Men*, the story of life at a New England school called Plumfield run by Jo March and her husband Professor Bhaer. Sitting at the window of her room in Rome and looking out at the statue of old

Louisa's nephews Frederick and John Pratt were the sons of her sister Anna and John Pratt. In 1887, Louisa legally adopted John so that he could manage her financial affairs and inherit the copyrights to her books after her death.

Triton in a fountain (usually with an icicle on his nose), she began to write of the adventures of a dozen boys and a few girls in a school which was run on the same principles as Bronson's Temple School in Boston when Louisa was a very little girl.

Into the novel she again put herself into Jo March Bhaer, who has matured into a "genial, comfortable kind of person" with a genius for understanding little boys and who still enjoys flying a kite. John Pratt is there as Meg's husband, John Brooke, as he was in *Little Women*. Abba and Bronson reappear as Mr. And Mrs. March as does May as the artistic Amy. Mr. Hyde—the naturalist who tickles lizards with straws, whistles to snakes, and tells tales about rocks and Indians—is based on Thoreau. The fun and games and tricks the children get up to are largely based on childhood experiences of the Alcott sisters and their friends.

As usual Louisa fell into "a vortex" of concentrated effort, and after three months of intense writing, it was relaxing to spend two weeks in Venice, cruising the canals in gondolas. Then they traveled to London where they settled in lodgings on Brompton Road. Louisa enjoyed showing May her favorite places and introducing her to friends. She also took care of business and an English edition of *Little Men* was published on May 15. Alice Bartlett left them after a pleasant year together, and Louisa began to think it was time for her to return also. Her books were earning enough so she could afford to pay for May to spend several more months studying art and sketching in England.

The trip back to New England on the *Malta* took twelve days. There was smallpox on the ship and Louisa's roommate came down with it. Although it was an anxious time, Louisa herself escaped infection and arrived home safely. In Boston she was met at the dock by her father and Mr. Niles in a carriage with a large red banner reading "Little Men: Life at Plumfield with Jo's Boys." Advance orders for the book were pouring in, and by the end of June, Roberts Brothers had printed 38,000

Abba Alcott in a study at Orchard House.

copies. Although *Little Men* never was as popular as *Little Women*, it too became a classic.

In Concord, Louisa was dismayed at how aged and feeble her mother looked, and she promised herself she would never go far away from her again.

Samuel J. May, Abba's brother and Louisa's uncle who had helped the Alcotts over the years.

8

Golden Goose

"Work is and always has been my salvation."
—Louisa May Alcott

A RETURN OF miserable aches and pains and dizzy spells spoiled Louisa's plans to work that summer. She went to the seashore, but the damp air increased her misery. The sudden death of Uncle Samuel in May only added to the gloom of the household. Abba was desolated by her brother's death, which left her the last living member of the family she grew up in. Bronson gave the eulogy at his brother-in-law's funeral, and Louisa called her uncle the "best friend of the family for years" who "made life sweet wherever he was."

In addition to poor health and housekeeping worries at Orchard House, too much company kept Louisa from the writing she was itching to begin. She decided to go to Boston to rest and try to get well. May was summoned back to run "the machine," as Louisa called the family home, and returned with stacks of paintings and cheerful tales of her adventures and of her "London lovers." Louisa hired two girls to help with the housework and installed a furnace to heat the drafty old house. Open fires were picturesque but inadequate during the long, cold New England winters. "Mother is to be cozy if money can do it," Louisa declared. "She sits in a pleasant room, with no work, no care, no poverty to worry her, but peace and comfort all about her." A long-cherished dream had come true.

Christmas at Orchard House was merry with a tree for her nephews, a family dinner, and games. Summarizing the year in her journal, Louisa said that on the whole it had been a good year in spite of pain. Last Christmas, she recalled, she and May had been in Rome, mourning the death of John Pratt. What would the next year bring? she wondered, adding, "I have no ambition now but to keep the family comfortable and not ache anymore."

One of Louisa's favorite mottos was, "All is fish that comes to the literary net." Now she set to work to prove it by turning her European travels into "bread and butter" in the form of sketches and stories. One of these stories, "Pelagie's Wedding," describes a French wedding she attended. She sold a series of travel articles called "Shawl Straps" to the *Christian Union*, and eventually expanded these sketches into a book that Roberts Brothers published as the second volume of her collected stories under the title *Aunt Jo's Scrapbag*.

When Louisa returned to Orchard House in June to help

May, she found herself besieged by fans and sightseers. She valued letters from children, parents, and teachers telling her that her books gave them pleasure and inspiration, and told a reporter, "This success is more agreeable to me than money or reputation." But she hated the intrusive curiosity that fame brought. "People *must* learn that authors have some rights," she complained. When reporters perched on the wall taking notes and strangers tried to interview her nephew Johnny as he played in the orchard, she was furious and declared that fame was definitely not a blessing.

Her parents, however, delighted in their daughter's celebrity and took every opportunity to brag about her. Bronson said he rode in his famous daughter's "chariot," and he used her name to promote his causes. In his lectures he referred to Louisa and quoted from her letters and her works. A poster announcing one of his "conversations" listed him as "The Concord Sage and Gifted Sire of Louisa May Alcott, Authoress of 'Little Women,' etc."

Although Louisa didn't like being referred to in this way, she used her influence to help him get his book *Concord Days* published by Roberts Brothers. She loved her impractical father deeply. When he left on one of his midwestern lecture tours in November, she was proud to see him leave "all neat and comfortable...in a new suit, overcoat, hat and all—like a gentleman." She, of course, had paid for the new clothes and for the new underwear, shirts, and gloves she packed into his new trunk. Remembering the "pathetic" old times when he had left in a shabby suit wearing mended shirts and socks, they laughed together with tears in their eyes.

When the editors of the *Christian Union* offered to pay her $3,000 for a serial story, Louisa pulled out an old manuscript titled *Success*, which she had begun many years ago. In it she included many of the experiences she had as she tried to earn a living and support her family. She

The Great Fire of Boston. Although the fire's effects devastated the city, Louisa's boardinghouse was spared.

changed the title to *Work* and again "plunged into a vortex" of effort as the story possessed her.

On November 9, 1872, tired from a hard day's work on the book, she was getting ready for bed when she heard sirens screaming and saw bright lights from her window. A young man burst into the boarding house yelling that Boston was on fire. Louisa bundled up and went to watch as leaping flames melted glass and great granite blocks of building stones like ice. The Common was stacked with huge heaps of goods dumped there by desperate shopkeepers who hired guards to watch over their merchandise. She saw "venerable Beacon Street gentlemen" fleeing the flames in coal carts piled high with books and others pushing wheelbarrows filled with their treasures.

The roaring flames created a whirlwind that sent blazing boards, bolts of cloth and rolls of paper flying in all directions, falling on roofs and spreading the fire. Trinity Church was burned along with other landmarks, and since water was ineffective in stopping the firestorm, firefighters began blowing up buildings. Louisa's boardinghouse was threatened, and she packed up her manuscript, a few books, her best gown, her new boots and was ready to flee, but the building was spared. The fire eventually spread over sixty acres in the business district of Boston, destroying some 3,000 stores, warehouses, and businesses. Louisa ended up with a mother cat and kittens that had been rescued by a friend. She later wrote a story called "Huckleberry" about an ugly, pitiful dog she saw howling amid the ashes of a burned house.

As 1873 began, the writing on *Work* was going well, although she had slowed her frantic pace for fear she would suffer a breakdown. Another thing that slowed her was the *way* she had to write it. Typewriters would not be sold commercially for another year; the first ones were clumsy machines, and Louisa never learned to use one. Since she needed to make three copies of her manuscript (one for the *Christian Union*, one for Roberts Brothers, and one for her British publisher) she wrote with a steel pen on "impression" paper. It required bearing down hard to make three readable copies. Her right thumb became permanently paralyzed from the pressure, and she taught herself to write with her left hand.

In February and March, Anna was dangerously ill with pneumonia, and Louisa went home to nurse her. While Anna was recovering, Louisa took Johnny back to Boston for a week. Despite these interruptions, she finished *Work* in April. May was tired of keeping house in Concord, and with her major project finished, Louisa moved back to Orchard House to take over. She gave May $1,000 and sent her to London to study for a year, glad to be able to help her talented sister and comforted as she "cleaned and grubbed" that May was free and happy.

Work, which was published in England and America in June, tells the story of Christie, a poor working girl who—like her creator—is bright, energetic, and independent. Struggling to earn an honest living, Christie works as a servant, a governess, an actress, a seamstress, and as a paid companion. After overcoming many obstacles, she marries David Sterling (another character modeled on Thoreau). When he is killed in the Civil War, Christie remains single, supporting herself and her young daughter by doing social work, helping young women find employment just as Abba Alcott had done when she worked in Boston. The book received good reviews and sold well, although it had nothing like the success of her juvenile books.

May stayed in London for almost a year and made good progress in her art studies. Her copies of the paintings of the famous British landscape artist J. M. W. Turner were highly praised and sold for $100. On her return, she and Louisa hung a number of her colorful landscapes to brighten the family home. Abba had developed heart problems and also had spells of mental confusion. The three sisters were concerned for the mother who had always been the one who took care of them all, and now they took turns being her caretaker.

In October, Louisa took rooms at the Bellevue Hotel on Beacon Street in Boston for the winter, so she could concentrate on writing. May commuted from Concord and used one of the rooms to give art lessons. Here Louisa began working on *Eight Cousins or The Aunt-Hill*. She told friends she was afraid it would be a dull story for her head was "not in it" and her bones ached most of the time. Publishers did not share her doubts about the unfinished book, for there was lively bidding to be the first to publish it. Louisa was amused and wrote in her journal, "The golden goose can sell her eggs for a good price, if she isn't killed by too much driving."

A painting of an owl by May Alcott. May was able to hone her artistic talents and study painting in Europe thanks to Louisa's financial support.

Eventually *Eight Cousins* appeared in twenty-five installments in the British magazine *Good Things* and in ten installments in *St. Nicholas* in America and was published as a book on September 25, 1875, simultaneously by Roberts Brothers and by the British publisher Sampson Low. The book tells the story of thirteen-year-old Rose Campbell who comes to live on the "Aunt Hill" after her beloved father dies. There she finds six aunts who have very different ideas of how to raise a girl, seven mischievous boy cousins, and a guardian uncle who has his own unconventional ideas about raising his ward. In the course of the book, Rose evolves from a timid semi-invalid into a healthy outgoing girl who can hold her own with her rowdy cousins. Her uncle helps her to realize she has as much right as they do to decide how she will live her life.

Like her mother, Louisa was deeply interested in promoting women's rights. She thought they should receive equal education and equal pay for equal work, and she ridiculed the nineteenth-century idea that men were supposed to be sturdy oaks and women clinging vines. She realistically admitted that there might be limitations to what a woman can do but urged ". . . in Heaven's name, give her a chance." She was involved in the suffrage movement, which sought to give women the right to vote in political elections. Over the years Louisa contributed many articles to the *Woman's Journal*, which was edited by her friend Lucy Stone, an outspoken social reformer.

In the fall of 1875 Louisa attended the Women's Congress held in Syracuse, New York, and after the speeches she was surprised by a sudden rush of girls with autograph albums and cards for her to sign. She wrote as long as her thumb and her patience held out. Then, she told Bronson, she "had to run for my life with more girls along the way and Ma's clawing me as I went."

From Syracuse she traveled to New York where she took rooms at the Bath Hotel, a kind of health spa, offering baths, massages, and health diets. New York welcomed the famous author, and she found the rapidly-growing city exciting. She attended meetings of Sorosis, a women's club devoted to helping women improve their lives. She was free from aches and worries and enjoyed parties and visits where she met celebrated artists, editors, actors and writers. She enjoyed riding in the newly-completed Central Park and attending plays. She also visited charitable institutions, helping prepare barrels of food and clothing for a school for freedmen in South Carolina.

She visited schools and jails and wrote a letter to her nephews describing a home for poor newsboys. There was a big schoolroom she told them with desks for 180 boys. Each boy paid six cents for a cubbyhole to store his things and five cents for supper. The boys, she told nephews Freddy and Johnny, were ragged but clean and happy to have this home to come to, as it was the only one they had. Each boy had a savings bank, and they were encouraged to save their pennies for their futures. Two brothers especially impressed her: Pete, a six-year-old and his nine-year-old brother who took care of him. "Think of that, Fred," she said. "How would it seem to be all alone in a big city, with no mama to cuddle you; no two grandpa's houses to take you in; not a penny but what you earned, and Johnny to take care of?"

On Christmas day she visited a children's hospital, where she handed out dolls to crippled children, and then went on to a mental hospital for children where she handed out hugs and toys. Although she received no presents herself that Christmas and missed both lunch and dinner, it was a memorable day for her when she recalled the delight on the faces of the children into whose hands she had placed gifts.

Much that she saw and experienced in New York would appear in stories and articles for both adults and children. By late January, tired of being a "fine lady" and anxious about her mother, she returned home. She and May gave the old house a grand spring-cleaning moving "two centuries" of dust. During the summer she took care of Abba, worked on short pieces, and waited for an inspiration to strike as to what her next book should be.

In late summer Mr. Niles suggested a sequel to *Eight Cousins*. He also suggested she let up on the moralizing—or preaching—that characterized her children's books and let the reader discover the moral for herself or himself as events unfold. Having been brought up by Bronson and Abba, Louisa found this advice impossible to follow and continued to be heavy-handed in spelling out the meaning of what happens in her stories. In the sequel *Rose in Bloom*, the cousins have grown up, and Rose is a thoroughly modern Victorian woman who staunchly supports the right of women to have lives outside their homes. She tells her cousins that women have minds and souls as well as hearts and insists, "We want to live and learn as well as love and be loved." Louisa wrote the book in September in four weeks. The first printing of 10,000 copies sold out in November. Her readers obviously were willing to overlook the preaching.

In the fall of 1876, Louisa sent May abroad to study for a year or two in London and Paris. Louisa was glad to pay for her sister's chance to follow her dream, and she was pleased when May wrote that she was working hard. In her journal Louisa wrote, "The money I invest in her pays the sort of interest I like. I am proud to have her show what she can do, and have her depend upon no one but me. My dull winter is much cheered by her happiness and success."

Her sister, Anna Pratt, had long wished for a home of her own for herself and her two boys in Concord. In the spring of 1877, Louisa helped her buy the Thoreau house on Main Street, and exhausted herself helping Anna move in. Tired and depressed she confided to her journal, "So she has *her* wish and is happy. When shall I have mine? Ought to be contented with knowing I help both sisters by my brains. But I'm selfish, and want to go away and rest in Europe. Never shall."

In 1877 someone at Roberts Brothers came up with the bright idea of publishing a series of books by well-known authors called the "No Name Series." Each

Did you know...

Orchard House in Concord, where the Alcotts made their home from 1858 to 1877, is over 300 years old. The Louisa May Alcott Memorial Association conducts tours and provides special exhibits and programs for visitors.

book was printed anonymously, and readers played a guessing game trying to figure out who wrote them. Louisa contributed a story called *A Modern Mephistopheles* in the racy style of her A.M. Barnard thrillers. It was sensational and romantic, and readers didn't dream it was written by the hallowed creator of *Little Women*. Louisa enjoyed the fun when friends told her they were sure she hadn't written that story because it was "just not her style."

As Abba's health deteriorated, Louisa suffered with her. It was hard to see her strong, energetic mother growing weak and feeble. When Abba felt well enough, Louisa took her on drives in the woods, stopping along the way to pick the flowers her mother loved. As she watched by Abba'a bedside, Louisa worried that the winter might be expensive, and she dashed off another children's book to pay for nurses and other possible necessities. *Under the Lilacs* tells the story of a boy and his dog who are runaways from a cruel life with a circus.

"Stay by me, Louy," her mother said, "and help me if I suffer too much." And Louisa did stay, even when she became so ill that it was feared she might die before Abba. In November both Abba and Louisa were moved to Anna's new home where they could be taken better care of. As Abba gradually weakened, her mind returned to her childhood, and she sometimes thought Louisa was her mother. On November 25, she died quietly in Louisa's arms. Louisa wrote to May that their mother had "a happy end with loving faces to look her last upon and tender hands to serve her."

She did not wish her mother back to suffer more, but wrote in her journal "A great warmth seems gone out of life."

Portrait of Louisa taken in the 1870s. Louisa continued to write many books despite her failing health, and even her doctor thought it was better for Louisa to write in order to rest than to sit idle and have her story ideas agitate her mind.

9

Foster Mother

"Hearts don't grow old."

—Louisa May Alcott

WITH ABBA'S DEATH, Bronson Alcott had lost his anchor, and Louisa had lost her dearest friend, the person who understood her passionate energy best because they were so much alike. Father and daughter drew closer together, and to ease their grief they began sorting through Abba's journals and letters with the intention of writing a memoir of her. But reading her record of the years of anxiety and struggle during her difficult life only increased their sadness, so they put her papers aside—and they never had the heart to write the memoir. Louisa did write a poem entitled "Transfiguration" in tribute to her mother. In it, she counted up the "treasures" her mother had left:

> Faith that withstood the shocks of toil and time;
> Hope that defied despair;
> Patience that conquered care;
> And loyalty, whose courage was sublime.

Abba had insisted that May not be sent for or told of her serious illness. May was making excellent progress in her career, and when one of her still life paintings was chosen to hang in a Paris salon, the family rejoiced with her. Abba refused to let her progress be interrupted, so May was far away when she learned of her mother's death. She wrote that a "tender friend" had consoled her in her grief. Ernest Nieriker, a handsome young Swiss banker, was the friend who offered her sympathy and distracted her by playing chess with her and by playing his violin for her. They both loved music and art and had many other tastes in common.

In February, May and Ernest became engaged, and on March 22, 1878, they were married at a private wedding in London. Louisa sent her sister $1,000 as a wedding gift and all good wishes for her new life. Ernest wrote to Bronson, who was pleased by his deep concern for May. Louisa was happy for her sister but couldn't help comparing their lives in her journal: "I so lonely, sad, and sick; she so happy, well and blest. She always had the cream of things, and deserved it. . . . I dawdle about, and wait to see if I am to live or die."

When the happy couple settled into a pretty house with a balcony and garden in northern France, they urged Louisa to visit them. She eagerly began making plans to go, but her health was poor, and when Anna broke her leg, Louisa postponed the trip to take care of the house, nurse her sister, and look after her nephews.

In January of 1879 Louisa moved to the Bellevue Hotel in Boston to begin work on a new book, *Jack and Jill*. She took time out to write and act in benefit performances of "Mrs. Jarley's Waxworks," adapted from Dickens' *Old Curiosity Shop*. Boston papers praised her witty performance and described in detail her fantastic costume, noting especially her bonnet which had a large feather that stood upright and gave "nodding emphasis to all her words." In her journal, Louisa wrote that she was getting too old for such endeavors, writing "A sad heart and a used up body make play hard work."

Anna's forty-eighth birthday on March 16 caused Louisa to reflect on her relationship with her oldest sister, calling her "The best woman I know, always reasonable, just, kind and forgiving." And she mused over how well they got along despite being so different. Louisa was concerned for her nephews' futures and invested $1000 for each of them to pay for their education. When May wrote that she was pregnant, Anna and Louisa spent many happy hours sewing together making "bibs and frocks" for the niece or nephew due to appear in November.

That summer Bronson achieved *his* dream by opening the Concord School of Philosophy. The sessions lasted four weeks and met in Orchard House. Anna and Louisa assumed the work of welcoming the students, providing food and tea, and cleaning and decorating the house before and after the sessions. Neither of them was much interested in the lectures and discussions. Anna said she preferred Louisa's philosophy "Do the duty that is nearest thee," and practical Louisa asked, "Why discuss the unknowable till our poor are fed and the wicked saved?" They resented the budding philosophers "roosting" on their steps but tried to look as if they enjoyed it

The Concord School of Philosophy. Bronson Alcott's dream of having his own school was finally realized in 1879.

for their father's sake. When the school ended in August, Louisa wrote "Hallylojah!" in her journal.

Another frustrating activity for Louisa that summer was her effort to interest the women of Concord in voting in the school committee elections. Women's suffrage had been a cause dear to Abba's heart, and Louisa also felt that classifying women with the "idiots and insane" who were not allowed to vote nationally was ridiculous. She organized meetings and drove from door to door trying to stir the women out of their rut. She herself set an example by being the first woman to register to vote in the election. She had little patience with the "timid and slow" women and decided her best contribution to promoting women's rights was in her writing, especially in the numerous pieces she wrote for the *Woman's Journal*.

As the end of May's pregnancy neared, Louisa's longing to be with her sister at the time of the birth increased. But "everyone" she knew advised her not to risk her health by going, and her common sense told her she might arrive an invalid herself and be more of a burden than a blessing to her sister. So instead she returned to the Bellevue to work on *Jack and Jill*. She could not work at her old hectic pace of fourteen hours a day and complained that the work was going slowly.

When news arrived that Louisa May Nieriker, or Lulu as she came to be called, had arrived safely on November 8, there was great rejoicing. The next news from France was not good. May was not recovering from the delivery; she had fever and was too sick to nurse her baby. "Oh, if I could only be there to help," Louisa moaned. "Such a tugging at my heart to be by poor May alone so far away."

The news grew worse. May was often unconscious and continued to lose strength. The family haunted the Concord post office looking for letters from France. Bronson was at the post office on December 31 when Mr. Emerson arrived at the house and handed Louisa a telegram from Ernest Nieriker telling of May's death. Ernest had sent the telegram to Emerson hoping he could help soften the blow for his friends, and he was right. "That hard moment," Louisa said, "was made bearable by the presence of this our best and tenderest friend."

In the nineteenth century, women were more apt to die in childbirth than they are today, and May had made careful preparations for that possibility. She had already expressed a desire for a simple funeral and burial in the quiet Montrouge Cemetery. And she had designated Louisa as the one to raise her namesake. May had written the family telling them not to mourn if she should die, as she had had two years of perfect happiness "such as few people know." In gratitude to Louisa for all she had done for her, May left her the pictures she had painted and her baby. "A precious legacy," Louisa called it and said that now she knew why she had lived—"To care for May's child and not leave Annie all alone."

The Alcott and Nieriker families found comfort in exchanging letters. Lulu was taken to stay with her grand-mother until the time was right for her to make the trip to America. Typically, Bronson and Louisa made verses to preserve May's memory. His was called "Love's Morrow" and Louisa's "Our Madonna." In it she called her sister a "golden-haired Madonna" and said of her:

> Rich colors on her palette glowed
> Patience bloomed into power;
> Endeavor earned its just reward,
> Art had its happy hour.

While she waited for Lulu's arrival, Louisa finished *Jack and Jill*, hoping her own personal misery didn't show in the story. Jill, an impulsive tomboy like Louisa, talks Jack into a dangerous sledding ride that ends in a near fatal accident. Jack's leg is broken and Jill's spine is seriously injured. During most of the story, which covers almost a year, she is forced to spend her time lying in bed or on a couch, and during her long convalescence learns to be wiser and more patient and to think more of others than of herself.

On August 21, Louisa sent a nurse to Europe to bring Lulu back. As she prepared a cozy nursery with a white crib, she thought anxiously of the "wide and terrible" ocean between her and her "treasure." On the day of her arrival in September, she waited eagerly on the wharf watching passengers disembark and wondering which of several

Louisa (Lulu) Nieriker, daughter of Louisa's sister May. She came to live with Louisa after May died.

babies might be hers. At last the captain appeared with "a little yellow-haired, blue-eyed thing" wrapped in white, and Louisa knew it was Lulu. Sophie Nieriker, the baby's French aunt, and the nurse were with the baby, but Lulu went immediately to Louisa and nestled against her. Louisa's heart was filled with pride and joy and love. The lively, happy baby soothed her grief as well as that of her Grandfather Bronson and Aunt Anna. "We all find life easier to like now the Baby has come," Louisa wrote.

She became so absorbed in the baby for several years that she found little time for anything else—not even for writing in her journal. She showered Lulu with kisses, hugs, toys and clothes, playing with her and telling her stories of "lambs, piggies, and kittens" by the dozens. It soon became clear that her niece had a personality much like Louisa's own, and her aunt reported that her child had "a strong will and quick temper, but very tender, generous and noble instincts."

On April 27, 1882, Ralph Waldo Emerson died, and Louisa said "Our best and greatest American gone." She had never forgotten her hero worship of him and the kindly way he had helped the family in their days of dire poverty by putting money "on a table under a book or behind a candlestick." He was doubly dear to her as her father's best and most support-ive friend and as the man who helped her most "by his life, his books, his society." Doorways in Concord were draped in black and the flags flew at half-mast. For his funeral, Louisa made a harp of yellow jonquils and helped decorate the church with pine branches and flowers. That night she stayed up until midnight writing an article on Emerson for the *Youth's Companion* so children would know what a great man he was. "A labor of love," she called it.

When the Concord School of Philosophy opened for its summer session, Louisa and Anna again assumed their roles as hostesses, cleaning women, decorators, cooks, and so on. One day Bronson asked them why they weren't attending the sessions, and Anna showed him a list with the names of 400 callers. Louisa reported, "He said no more."

The Hotel Bellevue had been converted into apartments, and Louisa went there in October to work on a book her publisher and fans had been begging her to finish. *Jo's Boys* was to be the sequel to *Little Men* and the final story about the March family. She had barely gotten started when a telegram arrived saying her father had had a paralytic stroke. She went home at once and found Bronson affected both physically and mentally. "It is so pathetic to see my handsome, hale, active old father changed at one fell blow into this helpless wreck," she wrote to a friend. He had written forty sonnets during the last winter, served as Dean of the School of Philosophy, and given fifty lectures. Enough, she said, to break down any man of eighty-three years. Out of her own experience she had frequently warned him against "overwork and taxation of the brain," but, like his daughter, he wouldn't listen to reason when he was possessed by an idea. During the first anxious days of his illness, Lulu was her greatest comfort. She felt she could bear anything with "this little sunbeam" to light up her world.

Bronson slowly improved, but he would never again be able to write and would always require nursing care. Louisa hired and fired a succession of unsatisfactory nurses, and she and Anna took turns taking care of their father. Just as Louisa had been pleased to be able to make her mother's last years comfortable, now she took pleasure in making her father's life as easy and pleasant as possible. Orchard House was sold, and Anna's house became the family home in Concord. Bronson's library was handsomely furnished, his books bound, and every comfort the sisters could think of provided. He was able to play checkers and read a little and enjoyed drives in the carriage Louisa provided. On his eighty-sixth birthday in 1885, Louisa wrote a long poem called "To My Father" in which she traced his life as a parallel to the journey that Christian made in *The Pilgrim's Progress*.

Ever since the publication of *Little Women*, Louisa had received a constant stream of letters from budding writers, fans, and teachers asking about her writing habits. She answered in her usual frank way, telling them she wrote quickly without polishing her work and needed only a pen and paper to do it. But, she added, each person must find his own method. She advised young people to "mind" their grammar, spelling and punctuation and to use short, strong, simple words. She told them to read the best books, see and hear good speakers, and talk with wise people to learn from them. She discouraged the letter-writers from pursuing authors as if they were idols, and told one teacher, "If you can teach your five hundred pupils to love books but to let authors rest in peace, you will give them a useful lesson and earn the gratitude of the long suffering craft, whose lives are made a burden to them by the modern lion hunter and autograph fiend."

In June of 1884, Louisa bought a cottage on Buzzards Bay in southern Massachusetts where she and Anna could take turns spending their vacations, and provide a place for the boys and Lulu to run free. Louisa, who never enjoyed cooking even after having done plenty of it, told a friend the cottage was without the "curse" of a kitchen, and they took their meals at a boardinghouse. Like her foster mother, Lulu was bold and curious. On her first experience with the ocean, she walked off toward Europe, and was up to her neck before she could be stopped. And she was annoyed that Louisa wouldn't let her go to the bottom to see the "little twabs." Louisa was proud of her "hearty, happy, natural child" and critical of nurses and nannies who didn't understand that "force and indifference" made Lulu naughty while "love and patience" made her easy to manage.

Louisa's own health was poor and she suffered from muscle pains, dizzy spells, headaches, hoarseness, indigestion, and sleeplessness. However, she still felt driven to write and to publish to make money for the family. One of her projects was a collection of her stories, which were published in *Spinning-Wheel*. She suggested to Mr. Niles that she gather together the little stories she told to Lulu and made into tiny books for her. He agreed and the stories were published by Roberts Brothers as *Lulu's Library* in a series that appeared in 1885, 1887, and 1889. When she felt well enough, Louisa pulled out the manuscript of *Jo's Boys* to resume work.

Now that her nephews Fred and Johnny were living and working in Boston, Louisa decided to find a house for the whole family in the city. After lengthy negotiations with real estate brokers, she took a large, furnished house in Louisburg Square. A study was fixed up for Bronson and a sunny nursery for Lulu and a playhouse in the yard. The family moved in on October 1, and Anna took charge of managing the housekeeping. Even so, it was hard for Louisa to be in the midst of so many people, and she sometimes longed for her solitary, quiet days in Boston.

Did you know...

Lulu Nieriker, Louisa's adopted niece, died in 1975 at the age of 96. Lulu had one daughter, six grandchildren and six great grandchildren.

In March of 1886, Louisa suffered a severe attack of vertigo and had sleepless nights for a week. But her head was working "like a steam engine." She planned her book on those "dreadful boys" (*Jo's Boys*) to the end, and longed to get up and write it. Her doctor finally agreed that it was best to let her get the ideas *out* so she could rest, but warned her to take it easy. She began writing for an hour or two a day and felt happy to live in her mind and forget her troublesome body for a time. In the summer, she sent Lulu off with Anna to the seaside cottage, and was able to finish the book in peace and quiet. It had long been eagerly awaited by her fans and orders poured in to Roberts Brothers, who planned a first edition of fifty thousand copies. Louisa felt it was not as good as it should have been because of the great intervals between the parts, but she consoled herself by remembering that "The children will be happy and my promise kept."

In this final book of the trilogy that began with *Little*

Women, Jo is middle-aged, the little men and women are married or pursuing careers, and Plumfield has become the kind of academy Bronson had wanted to establish. The last chapter, titled "Positively the Last Appearance," ends with the words, "Let the music stop, the lights die out, and the curtain fall for ever on the March family."

In June of 1887, Louisa made her will and legally adopted her nephew, John Pratt, who changed his name to John Pratt Alcott so that he could manage her financial affairs and inherit the copyrights to her books after her death. Her instructions were that he was to divide the income from them among his mother, brother, Lulu, and himself. Sophie Nieriker was to take charge of Lulu and return her to her family in France.

Dr. Rhoda Lawrence became Louisa's chief doctor, treating her with massage, diet, rest, and herbal remedies. Some years earlier Louisa had helped Dr. Lawrence buy "Dunreath Place," a home in Roxbury, Massachusetts that became a boarding house for patients, and the two women had become friends. Now Louisa moved into that home, where she received loving care. On her fifty-fifth birthday on November 29, 1887, she was showered with gifts and flowers. The numerous bouquets of flowers she received inspired the compilation of a book of her short stories called *A Garland for Girls*—the last book published during her lifetime.

On the first day of March 1888, Louisa felt well enough to go to see her father in Boston. She found him "very sweet and feeble." He kissed her and said, "Come soon." Two days later Bronson died, but Louisa did not know that her father was gone. On her return to Roxbury she complained of a violent headache and lapsed into unconsciousness. Two days later she died.

After a joint funeral service, Bronson and Louisa

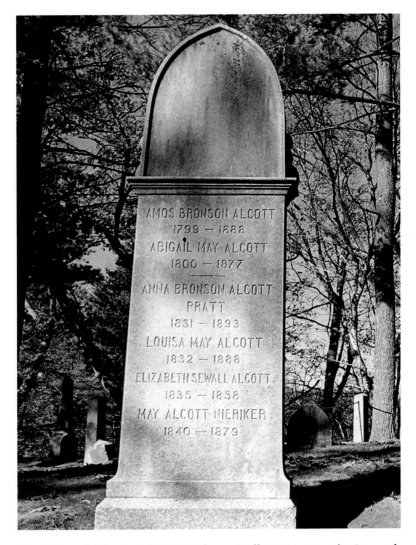

The Alcott family burial plot in Sleepy Hollow Cemetery in Concord. The Alcotts' friends Nathaniel Hawthorne, Henry David Thoreau and Ralph Waldo Emerson are also buried in this cemetery.

were buried with Lizzie and Abba in the Sleepy Hollow Cemetery. The pilgrim and his dutiful daughter had reached the Celestial City together. As Louisa had requested, her body was laid across the feet of her mother and father. The position aptly symbolizes her lifelong devotion to them.

1832 *Nov. 29:* Louisa May Alcott is born in Germantown, Pennsylvania

1834 Alcotts move to Boston, Massachusetts where Bronson Alcott opens his Temple School

1839 Temple School closes

1840 Alcotts move to Hosmer Cottage in Concord, Massachusetts

1843 *June to Dec.:* Alcotts live at Fruitlands experimental commune

1844 Louisa begins writing poetry, stories, plays, and keeping journal

1845–8 Alcotts purchase Hillside House, Concord

Louisa opens school in barn

1848 Alcotts move to Boston

Anna and Louisa teach school

1851 Louisa's poem "Sunlight" published in *Peterson's Magazine.*

1854 First book, *Flower Fables*, published

1856 Lizzie and May ill with scarlet fever

Alcotts buy Orchard House in Concord

1857 Lizzie dies

Anna and John Pratt announce engagement

"Love and Self Love" appears in *Atlantic Monthly*

1860 Anna and John marry

Louisa working on *Moods*

1861 Civil War begins

Louisa working on *Work*

1862 Louisa volunteers as nurse at Union Hotel Hospital in Washington

1863 "Pauline's Passion" wins $100 prize in competition

Louisa seriously ill with typhoid fever, returns home

"Hospital Sketches" printed serially and as book

1864 Publication of short stories and *Moods*

1865 Goes to Europe as nurse/companion to Anna Weld

1867 Becomes editor of *Merry's Museum*

1868 *Morning Glories*

Working on *Little Women*, Part I published in November

1869 Part II of *Little Women* published

1870 *An Old-Fashioned Girl* published in America and England

Louisa goes to Europe with May and Alice Bartlett

John Pratt dies

1871 *Little Men* published in America and England

Louisa returns home

1872 *Aunt Jo's Scrap-Bag*

1873 *Work*

1875 *Eight Cousins*

1876 *Rose in Bloom*

Louisa helps buy Thoreau house for Anna and her boys

1877 *A Modern Mephistopheles*

Mrs. Alcott dies

1878 May marries Ernest Nieriker in London

Under the Lilacs

1879 May dies following birth of Louisa May Nieriker

1880 *Jack and Jill* published

Louisa (Lulu) Nieriker arrives in Boston

1882 Ralph Waldo Emerson dies

Begins *Jo's Boys*

Mr. Alcott suffers paralytic stroke

1884 Orchard House sold

Buys cottage at Nonquitt

Spinning-Wheel Stories

1885 Leases house on Louisburg Square in Boston for family

Lulu's Library, Vol. 1

1886 *Jo's Boys* published

Moves to Dr. Rhoda Lawrence's home, Roxbury, Mass.

1887 *Lulu's Library*, Vol. 2

A Garland for Girls

Louisa's health deteriorates

1888 *March 4*: Mr. Alcott dies

March 6: Louisa dies

Little Women: Without a doubt the most popular of all of Alcott's books. It spawned an entire series as well as many film and television adaptations. The story of four sisters growing up in the 1800's finds resonance even today, but even while Alcott was alive, the subsequent stories of the March sisters never matched the popularity of the first novel. The 1994 film was a star-studded affair, starring Winona Ryder (who played Jo March), Susan Sarandon (as Marmee), Claire Danes (as Beth), and Kirsten Dunst (as Amy). However, the most famous actor to play Jo March was Katherine Hepburn in the 1933 film adaptation.

LITTLE WOMEN SERIES:

Little Women

Little Men

Jo's Boys

An Old-Fashioned Girl

Eight Cousins

Rose in Bloom

Under the Lilacs

Jack and Jill

OTHER CHILDREN'S BOOKS:

Flower Fables

Morning Glories

Lulu's Library (3 volumes)

SHORT STORY SERIES:

Spinning-Wheel Stories

Silver Pitchers

Proverb Stories

A Garland for Girls

Aunt Jo's Scrap-Bag

My Boys

Shawl-Straps

Cupid and Chow-Chow

My Girls

Jimmy's Cruise in the Pinafore

An Old-Fashioned Thanksgiving

ADULT NOVELS:

Hospital Sketches

Moods

Work

A Modern Mephistopheles

The Inheritance

COLLECTIONS OF "THRILLER" STORIES:

Behind a Mask

Plots and Counterplots

POEMS:

The Poetry of Louisa May Alcott

JOURNALS

The Journals of Louisa May Alcott. Edited by Joel Myerson & Daniel Shealy

LETTERS

The Selected Letters of Louisa May Alcott. Edited by Joel Myerson & Daniel Shealy

MEG (MARGARET) MARCH was based on Alcott's sister Anna. The eldest sister, Meg is pretty—which sometimes leads to vain behavior—and more domestic in nature. She also sometimes suffers from envy of wealth, especially as the Marches are not well-off.

JO (JOSEPHINE) MARCH was based on Louisa Alcott herself—free-spirited and independent, which often gets her into trouble. Tomboyish and headstrong, Jo acts as the head of the household while their father is away at war.

BETH (ELIZABETH) MARCH was based on Alcott's sister Lizzie. Sensitive and shy, Beth is always kind and willing to help others, but unfortunately falls ill to scarlet fever.

AMY MARCH was based on Alcott's sister May. Amy is an aspiring artist and selfish at times (she is the youngest March sister).

Bedell, Madelon. *The Alcotts: Biography of a Family.* New York: Potter, 1980.

Cheney, Ednah D. *Louisa May Alcott: Life, Letters, and Journal.* New York: Gramercy Printing, 1995.

Meigs, Cornelia. *Invincible Louisa.* Boston: Little, Brown, 1968.

Papashvily, Helen Waite. *Louisa May Alcott.* Boston: Houghton Mifflin, 1965.

Salyer, Sandford. *Marmee: The Mother of Little Women.* Norman: University of Oklahoma Press, 1949.

Saxton, Martha. *Louisa May Alcott: A Modern Biography.* New York: Farrar, Straus, and Giroux, 1995.

Stern, Madeleine B., ed. *Critical Essays on Louisa May Alcott.* Boston: G. K. Hall, 1984.

_____ . *Louisa May Alcott.* Norman: University of Oklahoma Press, 1985.

Ullom, Judith C. *Louisa May Alcott: A Centennial for "Little Women."* Washington: Library of Congress, 1969.

ELIZABETH SILVERTHORNE is the author of fifteen books and numerous articles and short stories for adults and children on a wide variety of subjects. She has written biographies of Marjorie Kinnan Rawlings, Sarah Orne Jewett, Anton Chekhov and of women in Texas medicine. This is her second book for Chelsea House. She lives in the village of Salado in the heart of Texas.